The United States Army W

The United States Army War College educates and develops while advancing knowledge in the global application of Land...

The purpose of the United States Army War College is to produce graduates who are skilled critical thinkers and complex problem solvers. Concurrently, it is our duty to the U.S. Army to also act as a "think factory" for commanders and civilian leaders at the strategic level worldwide and routinely engage in discourse and debate concerning the role of ground forces in achieving national security objectives.

SSI — The Strategic Studies Institute publishes national security and strategic research and analysis to influence policy debate and bridge the gap between military and academia.

CSL — The Center for Strategic Leadership and Development contributes to the education of world class senior leaders, develops expert knowledge, and provides solutions to strategic Army issues affecting the national security community.

PKSOI — The Peacekeeping and Stability Operations Institute provides subject matter expertise, technical review, and writing expertise to agencies that develop stability operations concepts and doctrines.

School of Strategic Landpower — The School of Strategic Landpower develops strategic leaders by providing a strong foundation of wisdom grounded in mastery of the profession of arms, and by serving as a crucible for educating future leaders in the analysis, evaluation, and refinement of professional expertise in war, strategy, operations, national security, resource management, and responsible command.

U.S. Army Heritage and Education Center — The U.S. Army Heritage and Education Center acquires, conserves, and exhibits historical materials for use to support the U.S. Army, educate an international audience, and honor Soldiers—past and present.

STRATEGIC STUDIES INSTITUTE

The Strategic Studies Institute (SSI) is part of the U.S. Army War College and is the strategic-level study agent for issues related to national security and military strategy with emphasis on geostrategic analysis.

The mission of SSI is to use independent analysis to conduct strategic studies that develop policy recommendations on:

- Strategy, planning, and policy for joint and combined employment of military forces;

- Regional strategic appraisals;

- The nature of land warfare;

- Matters affecting the Army's future;

- The concepts, philosophy, and theory of strategy; and,

- Other issues of importance to the leadership of the Army.

Studies produced by civilian and military analysts concern topics having strategic implications for the Army, the Department of Defense, and the larger national security community.

In addition to its studies, SSI publishes special reports on topics of special or immediate interest. These include edited proceedings of conferences and topically oriented roundtables, expanded trip reports, and quick-reaction responses to senior Army leaders.

The Institute provides a valuable analytical capability within the Army to address strategic and other issues in support of Army participation in national security policy formulation.

Strategic Studies Institute
and
U.S. Army War College Press

AT OUR OWN PERIL:
DOD RISK ASSESSMENT IN A POST-PRIMACY WORLD

Nathan P. Freier
Principal Author and Project Director

Christopher M. Bado
Christopher J. Bolan
Robert S. Hume
J. Matthew Lissner
Contributing Authors

Heather Bellusci
John R. Beurer
Ralph Borja
Steven Buelt
Michael Lechlitner
Robert D. Montz
Robert Phillips
Kelsey Smith
Contributing Researchers

June 2017

The views expressed in this report are those of the authors and do not necessarily reflect the official policy or position of the Department of the Army, the Department of Defense, or the U.S. Government. Authors of Strategic Studies Institute (SSI) and U.S. Army War College (USAWC) Press publications enjoy full academic freedom, provided they do not disclose classified information, jeopardize operations security, or misrepresent official U.S. policy. Such academic freedom empowers them to offer new and sometimes controversial perspectives in the interest of furthering debate on key issues.

*****

ISBN 978-1977877444

CONTENTS

Foreword ix

Acknowledgements xi

Executive Summary xv

Foundational Understanding 1

    I. Introduction: Post-U.S. Primacy and the New Fundamentals
       of Risk and Risk Assessment 3

    II. Study Methodology 13

Describing Risk 17

    III. The Logic of Post-Primacy Risk: Current Conventions
        and New Terms of Reference 19

Identifying Risk 39

    IV. Securing U.S. Position: Six Enduring Defense Objectives 41

    V. A Post-Primacy Decision-Making Environment 53

Assessing and Communicating Risk 67

    VI. A Post-Primacy Risk Concept: Diversity, Dynamism,
        Persistent Dialogue, and Adaptation 69

    VII. Communicating Risk: A Common Risk Currency 87

Study Outcomes 91

    VIII. Findings and Recommendations 93

    IX. Conclusion—Ownership, Culture, and Adaptation 103

Appendices 107

    Appendix I - Building the Principal Risk Portfolio:
          Illustrative Hazards and Demands 109

Appendix II - Expert Working Group (EWG) Participants 111

Appendix III - About the Contributors 113

FOREWORD

The U.S. Department of Defense (DoD) faces persistent fundamental change in its strategic and operating environments. This report suggests this reality is the product of the United States entering or being in the midst of a new, more competitive, post-U.S. primacy environment. Post-primacy conditions promise far-reaching impacts on U.S. national security and defense strategy. Consequently, there is an urgent requirement for DoD to examine and adapt how it develops strategy and describes, identifies, assesses, and communicates corporate-level risk.

A U.S. Army War College (USAWC) study team took on the risk issue specifically in July of 2016. This report outlines its findings. It opens a meaningful discussion on what enterprise-level risk identification and assessment should look like in the volatile post-primacy environment. It suggests that risk is the principal business of DoD's senior-most leadership. In addition, it further argues that corporate-level risk judgments at the strategic and military levels of analysis should revolve around a new post-primacy risk concept. That concept has four governing principles: **diversity**, **dynamism**, **persistent dialogue**, and **adaptation**.

According to the authors and the study team, diversity and dynamism populate and shape a sophisticated and structured risk dialogue. They further contend that the purpose of that dialogue is meaningful enterprise-wide adaptation to account for the most important and urgent hazards and demands emerging from the contemporary environment. Finally, the authors argue that high-level risk ownership, risk as a culture, and risk-based adaptation should be elevated as key pillars of DoD's contemporary strategy development ethos. All three concepts are vital to what the study's authors and researchers argue should be an inseparable and seamless strategy development and risk assessment process.

At Our Own Peril will be an important reference for the new Secretary of Defense, the Chairman of the Joint Chiefs of Staff (CJCS), the Service Chiefs, and the Combatant Commanders as they begin the collaborative process of strategy development over the next several months. It lays out in stark relief the advantages of a Department steeped in the language and business of risk, as well as the grave hazards associated with DoD relying on 20th-century strategy and risk conventions for insights on decidedly 21st-century challenges.

DOUGLAS C. LOVELACE, JR.
Director
Strategic Studies Institute and
U.S. Army War College Press

ACKNOWLEDGEMENTS

This report and its findings are the products of a U.S. Army War College (USAWC) faculty-student team who—over the course of 9 months—canvassed dozens of experts and thousands of pages of written material to arrive at a meaningful set of actionable findings and recommendations on the subject of risk and risk assessment in the context of contemporary U.S. defense strategy. The study's inspiration originates in the U.S. Army's "Fiscal Year 2017 Army Study Planning Guidance" and its priority interest in the components and high-level articulation of risk as it relates to and impacts senior-level Department of Defense (DoD) decision-making. As was the case with last year's report, *Outplayed: Regaining Strategic Initiative in the Gray Zone*, this study reflects a synthesis of insights, collective wisdom, and expert judgment of a universe of professionals with whom the team interacted over the past 9 months. We are extremely grateful for the cooperation and access afforded us throughout the research effort.

There are a number of individuals and organizations who deserve credit for the report's depth of analysis. However, well before identifying those whose insights were invaluable to the study's findings and recommendations, the team would first like to thank its four primary sponsors. First, this study was made possible by the active support of Headquarters, Department of the Army and its Strategic Plans and Policy Directorate. Further, the study team is also grateful for financial support originating in the Army Study Program Management Office.

As was the case with *Outplayed*, the study team recognized that the very best judgments on enterprise-level risk and risk assessment would require the backing and cooperation of not only the United States Army, but also further the Joint Staff and the Office of the Secretary of Defense (OSD). Thus, after gaining high-level Army support, the USAWC study team secured sponsorship from both the Office of the Deputy Assistant Secretary of Defense for Strategy and Force Development, as well as the Joint Staff, J-5.

The team is particularly grateful to the Joint Staff in this regard. After all, the USAWC study effort began just as the Joint Staff, J-5 was concluding its own Chairman of the Joint Chiefs of Staff Manual (CJCSM) 3105.01, *Joint Risk Assessment*. Far from being a distant or disinterested party in the USAWC study effort—especially given the recent completion of their own exhaustive survey of risk assessment—the study team's Joint Staff partners were enormously helpful in shaping and sharpening the report's focus and substance. It is the study team's sincere hope that J-5's participation in this study effort complemented and further informed their important work on risk. What is clear—from the study team's perspective—is that this report is far better because of J-5's persistent engagement and meaningful contributions throughout the study period.

In addition to the study sponsors, the USAWC study team heard from and incorporated a number of important outside perspectives from a wide variety of defense and military experts and stakeholders. Again, as was evident during the previous years' experience, this report's principal "consumers" or "customers" are the very defense and military staffs that are charged with responsible risk assessment and risk-informed decision-making on a daily basis.

Thus, among the myriad voices represented in this report, we are particularly grateful for the contributions of these hardworking defense and military professionals and honored that they considered this effort worthy of their time and intellectual energy. Among the aforementioned, we would single out the Joint and Service Staffs, U.S. Central Command (USCENTCOM), U.S. Special Operations Command (USSOCOM), U.S. Strategic Command (USSTRATCOM), U.S. Northern Command (USNORTHCOM), U.S. Pacific Command (USPACOM), U.S. Forces-Japan (USFJ), U.S. Army Pacific (USARPAC), and U.S. Pacific Fleet (PACFLT).

In addition to the significant number of U.S. defense and military staffs and headquarters the study team engaged, the report's findings were also shaped by encounters with senior and working-level U.S. Government representatives from the Office of the Director of National Intelligence (ODNI)/National Intelligence Council and the Defense Intelligence Agency (DIA). Further, several non-military organizations engaged the USAWC study team in lengthy roundtable discussions on the subject of risk and risk assessment. These included the American Enterprise Institute, the Center for Strategic and International Studies (CSIS), RAND Corporation, and the Institute for the Study of War.

Following a model tested and proven by last year's experience and to gain the widest possible set of running insights throughout the course of the project, the USAWC study team also again employed an expert working group (EWG) comprised of working-level stakeholders and professionals. EWG members committed to remaining engaged in the research effort from start to finish and offered meaningful insights both in formal meetings and in offline encounters. The EWG convened three times over 9 months, assisting the study team in refining the report's overall focus, substance, and findings.

The EWG included representatives from the American Enterprise Institute, Center for a New American Security; CSIS; JD Solutions Limited Liability Company (LLC); Joint Special Operations University; Joint Staff, J5; Marine Corps War College; Marine Corps Combat Development Command; McKinsey and Company; the Mitchell Institute; National Defense University/Institute for National Strategic Studies; OSD/Cost Assessment and Program Evaluation (CAPE); Office of the Deputy Assistant Secretary of Defense for Plans; Office of the Undersecretary of Defense for Intelligence; RAND; USAWC Department of Command, Leadership, and Management; the U.S. Senate Staff; Headquarters, Department of the Air Force; Headquarters, Department of the Army; Headquarters, Marine Corps; and finally, Headquarters, Department of the Navy.

In addition to the EWG, the USAWC study team was fortunate to receive the insights of a senior review group (SRG). This more experienced and distinguished strategic advisory group met during a single roundtable discussion at the conclusion of the project. Others in the SRG contributed "at range" as their schedules would not permit physical attendance at the group's only meeting. However, their contributions were no less important. In line with last year's approach, this year's SRG "stress-tested" the report's findings and recommendations to ensure they would enjoy the widest possible acceptance at the highest levels of defense and military decision-making. In effect, the SRG was the report's last "vote" prior to publication.

It is not an exaggeration to say that last year's SRG proved to be one of a handful of crucial ingredients to the wide success of *Outplayed: Regaining Strategic Initiative in the Gray Zone*. We anticipate the same holds true of this year's SRG. This year's SRG included Lieutenant General (LtGen) George Flynn, U.S. Marine Corps, Retired; Lieutenant General (LtGen) Wallace "Chip" Gregson, U.S. Marine Corps, Retired;

Dr. Frank Hoffman, National Defense University/Institute for National Strategic Studies; Rear Admiral (RADM) Sinclair Harris, U.S. Navy, Retired; Lieutenant General (LTG) Frank Kearney, U.S. Army, Retired; and Lieutenant General (Lt Gen) Chris Miller, U.S. Air Force, Retired.

Finally, in support of the EWG and SRG, the USAWC study team owes a debt of gratitude to the staff of National Defense University's Lincoln Hall and the Institute for National Strategic Studies. From a technical and logistical perspective, all working group meetings went off without a hitch because of their tireless efforts.

A final thank you is due to Dr. Kathleen Hicks, CSIS Senior Vice President, Henry A. Kissinger Chair, and Director of CSIS' International Security Program (ISP). This report received a high-impact public launch as a direct result of a strong strategic partnership between CSIS ISP and the USAWC. The report will no doubt benefit immensely from the support of CSIS' talented staff. In addition, for this, the USAWC study team is very grateful.

In the end, the analysis, findings, and recommendations of this report are those of the study team and its constituent members alone. Any errors of fact or logic are also the responsibility of the USAWC study team. Contributions of individuals and organizations should not be construed by the reader as an endorsement of all or part of the study's analysis, findings, or recommendations. We are very grateful to all including those listed in the previous paragraphs, as well as those responsible for report production behind the scenes. We believe all have made invaluable contributions to an important and timely discussion of **strategic** and **military risk** and risk assessment.

EXECUTIVE SUMMARY

INTRODUCTION

At Our Own Peril is the product of a year-long U.S. Army War College (USAWC) research effort. The report was sponsored by Army G-3/5 (Strategy, Plans, and Policy Directorate), the Joint Staff, J-5 (Strategy Development Division), and the Office of the Deputy Assistant Secretary of Defense for Strategy and Force Development. The work is intended to add to the inevitable debates on risk and risk assessment accompanying forthcoming defense strategy development.

The report endeavors to inform the defense strategy discussion by evaluating the components, high-level assessment, and articulation of risk by the Department of Defense (DoD) at the strategic and military levels of analysis, as well as across the operational and future challenges time horizon. Moreover, in doing so, it answers a single simple question: How should DoD adapt its current risk identification and assessment conventions to accommodate an environment defined by persistent, disruptive change?

To arrive at actionable findings and recommendations, the USAWC study team examined DoD's risk assessment challenge in four principal areas of inquiry: describing risk, identifying risk, assessing risk, and effectively communicating risk. The study team found three clear vulnerabilities or shortcomings in current risk convention. First, it is excessively focused on near-term military threats. Second, it lacks a meaningful connection back to concrete defense objectives. Finally, third, it has proven to be an insufficient catalyst for essential post-primacy defense innovation and adaptation. These are reflected in a general dissatisfaction among many DoD stakeholders on the state of risk as it relates to corporate-level strategy.

In response, this study recommends that risk become the persistent business of DoD's senior leadership. It further argues that corporate-level risk judgments should revolve around a new post-primacy risk concept and its four governing principles of diversity, dynamism, persistent dialogue, and adaptation.

DESCRIBING RISK

The imperative for fresh perspectives on enterprise-level risk and risk assessment emerge from the broad recognition of two adverse realities confronting the United States and its defense establishment. The first is the increasing vulnerability, erosion, and, in some cases, the loss of an assumed U.S. military advantage vis-à-vis many of its most consequential defense-relevant challenges. The second concerns the volatile and uncertain restructuring of international security affairs in ways that appear to be increasingly hostile to unchallenged U.S. leadership. *At Our Own Peril* identifies this new or newly recognized period as one of "post-U.S. primacy."

In the team's assessment, post-primacy has five interrelated characteristics:
- Hyperconnectivity and weaponization of information, disinformation, and disaffection;
- A rapidly fracturing post-Cold War status quo;
- Proliferation, diversification, and atomization of effective counter-U.S. resistance;

- Resurgent but transformed great power competition; and,
- Violent or disruptive dissolution of political cohesion and identity.

Individually and in combination, these post-primacy characteristics have extraordinary impacts on defense-relevant hazards and demands, and, by implication, enterprise-level risk and risk assessment. For strategists and senior defense decision-makers, the five post-primacy characteristics call for more dynamic, forward-looking, and adaptive approaches to both strategy development and risk assessment.

Consistent with current DoD practice and terms, the study team laid the conceptual foundation for their work by describing risk in four key dimensions: **military**, **strategic**, **operational**, and **future challenges**. The first two represent terminal ends on a vertical risk assessment continuum, whereas the latter two are similarly endpoints on a horizontal or time-based spectrum.

On the vertical continuum from top to bottom, **strategic risk** is the likelihood that DoD fails to effectively focus or define what the team calls DoD's principal risk portfolio. **Military risk,** on the other hand, involves judgments on the likelihood that DoD fails to adequately counter hazards to enduring defense objectives through the individual demands included in the portfolio. Along the horizontal time continuum, **operational risk** involves judgments on DoD's near-term vulnerabilities in the former two dimensions, and **future challenges risk** accounts for similar vulnerabilities over time.

IDENTIFYING RISK

After extensive engagement and consultation with defense and defense-interested communities of practice and interest, *At Our Own Peril* concludes that objectives-based vice threat-based risk assessment is most appropriate for post-primacy conditions. The study group surveyed 25 years of national security, defense, and military policy and identified six illustrative enduring defense objectives to apply against the current and future environment.

These objectives help senior leadership to determine the most appropriate strategic approaches to the environment's hazards and the specific military demands those approaches imply. The objectives are:
- Secure U.S. territory, people, infrastructure, and property against significant harm;
- Secure access to the global commons and strategic regions, markets, and resources;
- Meet foreign security obligations;
- Underwrite a stable, resilient, rules-based international order;
- Build and maintain a favorable and adaptive global security architecture; and,
- Create, preserve, and extend U.S. military advantage and options.

To be of the most utility, strategic and military risk assessment should identify the likelihood of failure or prohibitive cost in pursuit or defense of these enduring objectives, given an adopted strategy.

ASSESSING AND COMMUNICATING RISK

Post-primacy risk assessment has at its core the chief objective of enterprise-wide adaptation. The report concludes that this process begins with the identification of enduring objectives, strategy development in support of them, the identification of strategy-driven military demands, and determination of which of the demands are important and urgent enough to be included in the principal risk portfolio.

Like this articulation of objectives, the report identifies eight demands in the study's illustrative principal risk portfolio: Strategic Deterrence and Defense, Gray Zone/Counter-Gray Zone, Access/Anti-Access, Major Combat, Distributed Security, Influence/Counter-Influence, Counter-Network, and Humanitarian Assistance and Consequence Management. The eight demands do not represent the sum total of defense and military activity in specific operations or campaigns but, rather, their prevailing character.

The principal risk portfolio is the pacer against which DoD renders its most important risk judgments. Again, these judgments occur along the military/strategic and operational/future challenges axes. The study recommends the following four governing principles as central to any new post-primacy risk assessment process:

- **Diversity** in the number and types of hazards and defense demands considered. This requires DoD to adjust the "gold standard" for corporate risk assessment. While surge demand remains the principal risk driver, considerations of surge can no longer be limited to high-end combined arms warfighting.
- Acknowledgment of the inherent **dynamism** of DoD's contemporary decision-making environment and its impact on both defense-relevant hazards and DoD's response options. This includes accounting for inevitable changes in the importance and urgency of hazards and demands, as well as DoD's projected capability, capacity, and agility to respond effectively to fluid environmental change.
- **Persistent dialogue** on enterprise-level risk and risk management. In short, the study team argues that senior DoD and military leaders should engage directly in a deliberate, sophisticated, and structured risk discussion that accounts for and adapts to the environment's inherent diversity and dynamism.
- Finally, a commitment to constant and unrelenting risk-based defense **adaptation** as a by-product of the aforementioned persistent dialogue.

The study team suggests that this simple parsimonious post-primacy risk construct of **diversity, dynamism, persistent dialogue**, and **adaptation** offers new opportunities for senior defense leaders to communicate meaningful insights in a new common risk currency. On more than one occasion, the study team heard that the contemporary language of risk was stale.

In response, the report suggests that senior leadership use this uncomplicated but still sophisticated construction as the principal vehicle for risk communication. Naturally, use of this format must be preceded by clear and unambiguous articulation of enduring defense objectives, important and urgent hazards, surge demands, and adopted or proposed strategic courses of action. These are stage-setting terms of reference for the wider risk discussion that follows.

FINDINGS AND RECOMMENDATIONS

The study identifies four major findings and six associated recommendations for consideration by senior DoD leadership:

Findings

- Contemporary defense strategy development and risk assessment will occur under post-primacy circumstances.
- Enterprise-level risk does not exist absent meaningful intentions, strategic objectives, or courses of action.
- Enterprise-level risk assessment should be an uncomplicated but not unsophisticated dialogue.
- Post-primacy strategic conditions will demand more federated approaches to risk assessment.

Recommendations

- Adopt an objectives-based vice threat-based approach to enterprise-level risk assessment.
- Build a strategy-focused risk concept around four governing principles: diversity, dynamism, persistent dialogue, and adaptation.
- Pace DoD's risk assessment against a principal risk portfolio.
- Issue stand-alone, secretary-level risk guidance as a part of the strategy development process.
- Integrate interagency insights into DoD's risk assessment and "lead-up" as trusted partners toward a common "whole of government" risk picture.
- Integrate core allies and partners into the risk assessment process.

THE WAY AHEAD

Over the course of 9 months of intensive research and engagement with defense-focused communities of interest and practice, the USAWC study team arrived at the aforementioned actionable findings and recommendations for senior defense leadership. The team recognizes that the findings and recommendations only represent the first steps in what should be a more comprehensive, whole of government, risk assessment concept.

The need for greater interagency integration on subjects like risk is a constant refrain across multiple issue areas. It will not be solved overnight. Nonetheless, this study makes clear recommendations on how DoD might start the process. First, it suggests integrating interagency insights into DoD's risk assessments. By doing so, it may in fact demonstrate the value of risk-based decision-making to the rest of the American national security community.

In the final analysis, the study team suggests three foundational insights will also guide DoD toward higher ground on 21st-century risk identification and assessment. These insights involve: **risk ownership**, **risk as a culture**, and **risk as an instrument for enterprise-wide adaptation**. On the first, the study team suggests that strategic guidance and risk judgments will only permeate DoD and inform all senior leader decision-making to the extent that responsibility, authority, and ownership of risk are unambiguously aligned. As the most senior DoD officer in the chain of command, the study suggests that corporate-level risk leadership in this regard lies squarely in the hands of the Secretary of Defense.

The second insight focuses on **risk as a culture**. The study team found that risk identification and assessment could not simply be a process, a product, or a static judgment on hazard or danger. It needs to be a persistent component of DoD's corporate culture. In short, risk identification and assessment need to be pervasive elements of DoD's strategic dialogue and remain central to all consequential DoD decision-making.

Finally, as for **risk as an instrument of adaptation**, the findings are unequivocal. Any and all corporate-level risk identification and assessment within DoD must have as its expressed purpose, adaptation to ever-changing strategic circumstances. The study team outlined a risk concept with four governing principles: diversity, dynamism, persistent dialogue, and adaptation. The report argues that the last is the most important among them. If risk assessment is not linked to meaningful adaptation, then it is a wasted exercise.

In the end, this study argues for a corporate risk model founded on persistent senior leader dialogue. The concept should be fine-tuned to monitor and adapt to persistent change in strategic conditions, offering senior leadership clear strategic choices. Maintenance of U.S. defense and military advantage are at stake in the process. DoD's future risk concept should proceed from that weighty and potentially grave point of departure. Short of that, DoD exposes current and future performance to significant unrecognized or under-recognized hazard.

FOUNDATIONAL UNDERSTANDING

I. INTRODUCTION:
POST-U.S. PRIMACY AND THE NEW FUNDAMENTALS OF RISK AND RISK ASSESSMENT

> In the environment we are in today, with the complexity and volatility and variety of challenges we have, how do we assess risk?[1]

In light of seismic changes in the international system and the impact of those changes on U.S. national security interests, there is an urgent requirement for the U.S. Department of Defense (DoD) to examine how it describes, identifies, assesses, and communicates risk. This report begins that process and suggests that corporate risk judgments at the **strategic** and **military** levels of analysis should emerge from a persistent, sophisticated, and structured risk dialogue at the highest levels of DoD decision-making.[3] That discussion should center on four important risk principles: requisite **diversity** in the hazards and responses considered, acknowledgment of the inherent **dynamism** of DoD's contemporary decision-making environment, persistent high-level dialogue on risk and risk management, and a commitment to risk-based defense **adaptation** as a by-product of that persistent dialogue. In the end, risk identification and assessment are inherent components of effective enterprise-level strategy development and strategic adaptation.

Across . . . categories of risk, organizations should seek to identify minimally acceptable levels of capacity and performance in the capabilities it determines are necessary to secure organizational objectives. This is accomplished through stress-testing the strategy, identifying breaking points and assessing impacts to organizational objectives.[2]

Separating risk from the business of strategy invariably hazards two undesirable outcomes. The first is "failure" or the pursuit of objectives or policy goals that prove overly ambitious or unattainable in practice. The second is "prohibitive cost." This marks a pursuit of objectives or goals that in the end prove little more than Pyrrhic victories, robbing DoD of depth or freedom of action to pursue other—often more important—future ends.[4] According to the 2005 *National Defense Strategy* (NDS), where these terms originated:

> We assess the likelihood of a variety of problems—most notably, failure or prohibitive costs in pursuit of . . . objectives. This approach recognizes that some objectives, though desirable, may be unattainable, while others, though attainable, may not be worth the costs.[5]

The imperative for fresh perspectives on enterprise-level risk emerges from broad recognition of: 1) the vulnerability, erosion, or even loss of assumed U.S. military advantage vis-à-vis many of its most consequential defense-relevant challenges, and 2) a volatile restructuring of international security affairs that appears increasingly inhospitable to unchallenged American leadership.[6] On both counts and in the words of one member of the study's expert working group (EWG), contemporary risk assessment should start from the jarring realization that "we can lose."[7] The U.S. military hazards sacrificing core interests and objectives, global position, and material capability if it does not act now to have a greater appreciation for military- and strategic-level risk in the contemporary environment.

Indeed, this study argues that the volatile restructuring of international security affairs currently underway marks the American entrance into a third transformational era since the end of the Cold War. In addition, it is an era that the U.S. defense enterprise is ill-equipped to contend with from a risk perspective. The first of the preceding two eras is commonly referred to as the "post-Cold War" period, a time where the United States and its military benefited from unprecedented reach and advantage vis-à-vis the nearest or most threatening of its state rivals. The second era can most reasonably be described as the "post-9/11" period. It saw the United States and its defense establishment suffer a disruptive "strategic shock."[9]

> *The 17-year period after the Cold War . . . was a unique time when American power was essentially unchallenged. . . . we have been moving into a new era—a period of enhanced global competition, and the acceleration of trends that challenge our preeminence, complicate our decision-making, and demand of us greater agility and geopolitical savvy.*[8]

That shock exposed both the vulnerability engendered by dogged adherence to longstanding national security bias and convention, as well as inherent American adaptability to fundamental change in strategic conditions. Each of these eras presented defense and military leaders with unique risk considerations. Each also offered contemporary decision-makers with clues as to how they should identify, describe, and assess contemporary risk going forward.

Now, it is becoming increasingly clear that the United States is either at the doorstep or in the midst of a third—even more uncertain—wave of foundational strategic change. This study labels this period "post-primacy." For DoD, post-primacy is marked by five interrelated characteristics:

- Hyper-connectivity and weaponization of information, disinformation, and disaffection;
- A rapidly fracturing post-Cold War status quo;
- Proliferation, diversification, and atomization of effective counter-U.S. resistance;
- Resurgent but transformed great power competition; and finally,
- Violent or disruptive dissolution of political cohesion and identity.

While the United States remains a global political, economic, and military giant, it no longer enjoys an unassailable position versus state competitors. Further, it remains buffeted by a range of metastasizing violent or disruptive nonstate challengers, and it is under stress—as are all states—from the dispersion and diffusion of effective resistance and the varied forces of disintegrating or fracturing political authority. In brief, the status quo that was hatched and nurtured by U.S. strategists after World War II and has for decades been the principal "beat" for DoD is not merely fraying but may, in fact, be collapsing. Consequently, the United States' role in and approach to the world may be fundamentally changing as well.[10]

This new post-primacy period is distinct from either of the previously mentioned eras. Moreover, it is laden with profound implications for DoD and its civilian and military leadership. Consequential global events will happen faster than DoD is currently equipped to handle. U.S. defense capabilities and concepts will rarely be a perfect fit for the conditions they encounter. Indeed, while the United States remains a global military power, it no longer can—as in the past—automatically generate consistent and sustained local military superiority at range. Finally, the complexity of DoD's decision-making and operating environments will increasingly defy its current strategy, planning, and risk assessment conventions and biases.

In short, most of the instruments, approaches, concepts, and resources that have historically either helped the U.S. defense enterprise generate advantage or adapt to change are likely not keeping pace with the strategic change afoot in the post-primacy era. Thus, American senior leaders and strategists will have to simultaneously design, build, and persistently adapt strategic responses to an environment where the one certainty is in fact uncertainty. The defining quality of that profound uncertainty is constant, meaningful change in strategic and operational conditions. Thus, DoD requires a nimble and adaptive risk assessment and management approach that rivals DoD's exogenous decision-making environment in its inherent proclivity for adaptation and change.

In addition, for the foreseeable future, all of DoD's risk-informed choices will occur under pressure from post-primacy's transformational strategic forces and conditions. In the end, the origin, character, complexity, scale, and variety of post-primacy defense-relevant hazards and associated military demands require fresh perspectives on the "fundamentals" of defense risk and risk assessment. This study does just that in four principal areas of inquiry.

FOUR PRINCIPAL AREAS OF INQUIRY: DESCRIBE, IDENTIFY, ASSESS, AND COMMUNICATE

To arrive at an actionable set of findings and recommendations, the U.S. Army War College (USAWC) study team set out to create a new baseline perspective on DoD's post-primacy risk and risk assessment challenges. The study effort tackles the risk challenge in four principal areas of inquiry: **describing risk, identifying risk, assessing risk**, and **effectively communicating risk**. In the end, the study team is confident that its work complements recent Joint Staff work and independently makes meaningful contributions to future risk-informed strategy and policy development.

First, this study identified touchstones for describing risk at the strategic and military levels of analysis. These two risk bins are codified in enterprise-level DoD deliberations via nearly 2 decades of legislation and Pentagon policy.[11] As a result of its investigation, the study team developed descriptions (not definitions) of strategic and military risk that depart from current DoD or Joint Staff convention. However, they do so thoughtfully and in accordance with first principles that see risk as some "probability . . . of damage, injury, liability, loss, or negative occurrence that is caused by external or internal vulnerabilities."[12]

The study's adapted view of strategic and military risk is intended to provide senior defense and military leaders with a common launch point for assessing and communicating the "nature and magnitude" of post-primacy risk.[13] As important, the descriptions of strategic and military risk outlined in the next sections provide the requisite connective tissue between the two levels of analysis. In this regard, the study team concluded that strategic and military risks are terminal points at two ends of a single risk continuum and not wholly separate and distinct considerations.

5

The descriptions of strategic and military risk provided in the report's next section account for anticipated 10-year DoD surge demands while not necessarily dogmatically adhering to past defense bias and convention. Indeed, the study team found that the same deeply embedded defense bias and convention may both undermine a common, meaningful, and contemporary perspective on risk and also prevent effective enterprise-level risk assessment at both the strategic and military levels of analysis. In short, neither current defense convention, nor the strategy development and planning it informs may adequately account for a dynamic post-primacy security environment awash in new-age defense-relevant challenges and associated military demands.

In the second and third areas of inquiry and consistent with the work of Dr. Michael Mazarr of RAND, the study team acknowledges that risk identification and risk assessment—at both the strategic and military levels of analysis—are less the products of mathematical formulas and more the artful organization of frameworks for thoughtful risk allocation and apportionment within and between various strategic choices.[14] The team found that this perspective on risk gives senior defense and military leaders the freedom to develop and adapt innovative outlets for negotiating responses and remedies to identified risks.[15]

In the end, the study team concluded that a broad, simple, parsimonious, and adaptable concept for assessing prospects for either failure or prohibitive cost in pursuit of defense objectives would yield more meaningful enterprise-level decisions. Indeed, the alternative risk concept discussed in detail later offers senior leadership a tangible framework for weighing and adopting one or more of the four risk management paths widely codified in professional literature on the subject.[16] These include avoiding risk, mitigating risk, transferring risk, or accepting identified risk outright and proceeding with an adopted course of action with the full knowledge of its existence and potential impact.[17]

On the third line of inquiry, specifically assessing risk, the study team constructed an alternative DoD risk concept founded on four important foundational principles. These include: diversity in the hazards and demands considered; recognition of the inherent dynamism of DoD's decision-making environment; **persistent dialogue** among senior DoD leaders about the relationship between at-risk objectives, the hazards to them, the demands associated with their security, and internal/external institutional priorities; and finally, adaptation to identified risks as a by-product of persistent dialogue.

A consistent observation by those the study team engaged throughout the research effort involved widespread doubt about the degree to which current risk conventions actually resulted in real changes in strategy, strategic plans, concepts, and structural or material solutions. Thus, adaptation became a late and important addition to the alternative risk concept recommended in the report.

The concept of adaptation focuses risk assessment more clearly on outcomes. In short, adaptation to positive and negative change in the decision-making or operating environments is in fact the point of any honest and meaningful risk assessment exercise. Adaptation implies both effectively communicating the risks associated with an adopted strategy or course of action, as well as acting according to best judgment to lower the impact of any and all identified hazards through change.

In the forthcoming analysis, the study team suggests that risk assessment is a layered dialogue that accounts for and categorizes the most important defense-relevant hazards, their relationship to enduring defense objectives, and the demands those relationships imply. Once identified, the demands are collected in what the study team calls DoD's **principal risk portfolio**. The **importance** of identified demands relative to objectives and priorities, as well as the **urgency** associated with addressing them determines both the contents of the risk portfolio and prioritization among its identified demands. Initially, this occurs simultaneous to or in concert with strategy development. In addition, the study suggests it subsequently occurs in the process of persistent routine strategic assessments as well.

The principal risk portfolio and its constituent demands then become the pacing instruments for strategic and military risk assessment. The portfolio should reflect both the inherent diversity of DoD's potential pacing hazards and demands, as well as the dynamism of contemporary strategic conditions. Once the portfolio is established, the study suggests that DoD persistently assesses both overall and demand-specific risk in six basic areas applicable to both the strategic and military levels of analysis.[18] These six considerations become the focal point of a persistent risk-based dialogue at senior levels of DoD.

Finally, on the subject of communicating risk effectively, the study team found that once identified and assessed, risk is best communicated in terms of the common "risk currency" used to arrive at key enterprise-level risk-related judgments—diversity, dynamism, dialogue, and adaptation. That common currency first leverages the principal risk portfolio and its consideration of urgency, importance, capability/capacity, and agility. It then integrates that portfolio and its constituent demands into a strategy-focused dialogue where senior-level risk judgments emerge and are communicated consistently across the enterprise.

WILL NOTS, WILLS, AND WAY AHEAD

This report will not pass judgment on current DoD or Joint risk assessments. Its primary purpose is to provide a fresh set of first principles on the topic of defense-relevant risk and risk assessment. It will not directly assess contemporary DoD risk judgments. It will further not directly critique the current joint risk assessment process outlined in great detail in the Chairman of the Joint Chiefs of Staff Manual (CJCSM) 3105.01, *Joint Risk Analysis*.[19] That process for the time being is being codified and promulgated across DoD.

What the report does do is add to the inevitable debate on risk and risk assessment that will accompany forthcoming defense strategy development. As suggested, the report will also make meaningful recommendations in four broad and important issue areas: describing, identifying, assessing, and communicating risk. Over the course of the forthcoming nine sections, the report will address these by outlining a logical case of vetted concepts, culminating in a set of four major findings and six specific actionable recommendations.

Practically, the report takes the four lines of inquiry and analysis of them and presents them in four major segments: 1) describing risk, 2) identifying risk, 3) assessing and communicating risk, and finally, 4) study outcomes. These segments are further broken down into nine individual sections. After the introductory discussion presented here in Section I, Section II describes the specific methodology employed to arrive at the study's findings and recommendations.

Section III opens a discussion on describing risk. It outlines both current DoD risk convention, as well as an independent perspective on foundational study terms of reference. A key task in Section III is describing the study team's conceptions of strategic and military risk and their relationship to the post-primacy decision-making environment. As in the case of last year's gray zone report, Outplayed: Regaining Strategic Initiative in the Gray Zone, the study team decided to describe strategic and military risk vice define them in order to leave senior defense and military leaders reasonable latitude to adapt the concepts to inevitable changes in context and priorities.[20]

As it builds toward descriptions of strategic and military risk, Section III progressively introduces study team interpretations of a number of foundational concepts used throughout the report such as: surge, **operational** and **future challenges risk**, as well as a more fulsome description of the **principal risk portfolio**. The concepts and descriptions in this section provide the study's consumers with an introduction to the common "risk currency" employed throughout the report.

Section IV opens the discussion of describing risk. It identifies six **enduring defense objectives**. After an intensive survey of U.S. defense and national security convention over the past 25 years, the team concluded that the six objectives outlined in Section IV capture best advice on the likeliest potential drivers for U.S. military surge demand over the next decade. In the study team's view, the objectives are the principal touchstones for gauging the relative importance of key defense-relevant hazards, designing a realistic strategic approach to secure interests and objectives against them, and identifying the broad military demands associated with fulfilling that strategy.

Section V continues the discussion of identifying risk. It responsibly and independently surveys the post-primacy decision-making environment. It identifies five core characteristics of post-primacy circumstances that the team believes best inform DoD's 10-year strategic azimuth. In this regard, the study team took the advice of a high-ranking allied military strategist who observed that effective risk identification and assessment is "all about [the] working assumptions" employed to inform strategy development and strategic planning. In the end, the characteristics outlined in Section V are in fact foundational assumptions the study team suggests will drive DoD decision-making at least through the next decade. They provide the context within which hazards to enduring defense objectives and pacing 10-year defense demands are identified and collected in the report's postulated principal risk portfolio.

Section VI begins a discussion on assessing and communicating risk. It offers senior DoD decision-makers with an alternative risk concept founded on the four principles of: diversity, dynamism, persistent dialogue, and adaptation. In many respects, diversity and dynamism are first demonstrated in descriptions of the principal risk portfolio, and the concept of persistent dialogue largely rests on structured discussions of six important risk considerations. Adaptation synthesizes the best information emerging from the first three principles and is the process by which DoD accounts for changes in its strategic and military risk profile.

Section VII provides a brief discussion of effective risk communication. In general, the study concludes that risk communication is the process by which adaptation begins. It is grounded in the common currency of diversity, dynamism, and persistent dialogue. In addition, it employs the six strategic and military risk considerations and principal risk portfolio to carry a sophisticated risk discussion from the confines of "The Tank" to a broader set of important risk-interested stakeholders.[21]

Section VIII begins articulation of the study outcomes. It describes the study's actionable findings and recommendations. There are four major findings and six key recommendations. The study team considers the findings and recommendations additive to ongoing work. However, where necessary, the study team recommends transformational change in DoD practice. In the end, the study team strongly believes that adoption of the findings and recommendations will change the way senior leadership looks at their post-primacy risk challenges. The team suggests that its findings and recommendations are particularly useful now as DoD endeavors to conduct a compressed strategy development process over the summer.

The report concludes in Section IX, where the study team provides final insights on how DoD might reimagine a more effective and meaningful risk and risk assessment convention—especially now in the midst of strategy development.[22] Admittedly, this report is yet another vote among many on the subjects of risk and risk assessment. However, it is also an analysis born of engagement with the widest possible set of risk-conscious stakeholders operating inside or in support of the defense enterprise. Their voices are embedded throughout and this study is the result of their collective wisdom and best judgment.

In the end, the report's principal goal is to advise senior defense and military leadership on how they might—in a more broadly consumable way—describe, identify, assess, and communicate post-primacy risk. It seeks to establish a common, cogent, and adaptable risk currency. That currency should carry key risk considerations from strategy development and risk identification to effective risk communication and persistent risk assessment. It also seeks to align the risk perspectives of senior defense and military leadership with that of the important non-DoD constituencies most concerned with DoD's risk-based choices. The forthcoming section opens this endeavor by outlining the study methodology.

ENDNOTES – SECTION I

1. General Joseph F. Dunford, as quoted in Jim Garamone, "Dunford Details Implications of Today's Threats on Tomorrow's Strategy," DoD News, August 23, 2016, available from *https://www.defense.gov/News/Article/Article/923685/dunford-details-implications-of-todays-threats-on-tomorrows-strategy/*, accessed April 24, 2017.

2. U.S. Special Operations Command (USSOCOM), "Risk Concept Paper," unpublished staff paper provided to the study team on a visit to USSOCOM headquarters at MacDill Air Force Base, FL, January 17, 2017.

3. See *Quadrennial defense review*, 10 U.S.C. § 118 (2014), available from *https://www.gpo.gov/fdsys/pkg/USCODE-2014-title10/html/USCODE-2014-title10-subtitleA-partI-chap2-sec118.htm*, accessed April 4, 2017; Michael J. Mazarr, "Rethinking Risk in Defense," War on the Rocks, April 13, 2015, available from *https://*

warontherocks.com/2015/04/rethinking-risk-in-defense/, accessed May 10, 2017; and Michael J. Mazarr, "Fixes for Risk Assessment in Defense," War on the Rocks, April 22, 2015, available from *https://warontherocks. com/2015/04/fixes-for-risk-assessment-in-defense/*, accessed May 10, 2017. The terms "strategic" and "military" risk as levels of analysis have been common to the Department of Defense (DoD)/legislative language for some time. In addition, RAND Corporation's Michael J. Mazarr has been the defense analytic community's most recent influential and thoughtful voice on the topic of risk as iterative dialogue vice overly formulaic process.

4. See Donald Rumsfeld, *The National Defense Strategy of the United States of America*, Washington, DC: U.S. Department of Defense, March 2005, available from *archive.defense.gov/news/Mar2005/d20050318nds1. pdf*, accessed April 22, 2017, pg. 11. The principal author of this report was one of the contributors of the 2005 *National Defense Strategy* (NDS). In the course of strategy development, the terms "failure" or "prohibitive cost" were introduced into DoD risk lexicon.

5. *Ibid.*

6. General Martin Dempsey, *The National Military Strategy of the United States of America 2015*, Washington, DC: U.S. Joint Chiefs of Staff, June 2015, available from *www.jcs.mil/Portals/36/Documents/Publications/2015_National_Military_Strategy.pdf*, accessed April 4, 2017; National Intelligence Council, *Global Trends: Paradox of Progress*, Washington, DC: National Intelligence Council, January 9, 2017, p. 6, available from *https://www.dni.gov/index.php/global-trends-home*, accessed January 14, 2017.

7. This quote came from a senior service participant in the first expert working group (EWG) at the National Defense University in Washington, D.C. on July 22, 2016.

8. Former Director of the Central Intelligence Agency (CIA) John E. McLaughlin, "The State of the World: National Security Threats and Challenges," Statement before the Committee on Armed Services, Washington, DC: U.S. House of Representatives, February 1, 2017, available from *docs.house.gov/meetings/ AS/AS00/20170201/105509/HHRG-115-AS00-Wstate-McLaughlinJ-20170201.pdf*, accessed April 24, 2017.

9. Nathan Freier, "Known Unknowns: Unconventional 'Strategic Shocks' in Defense Strategy Development," Carlisle, PA: Strategic Studies Institute, U.S. Army War College, November 2008, p. 2, available from *ssi.armywarcollege.edu/pdffiles/PUB890.pdf*, accessed April 4, 2017.

10. National Intelligence Council, p. 6.

11. *Quadrennial defense review*, 10 U.S.C. § 118(a)(2)(G) (2011), available from *https://www.gpo.gov/fdsys/ pkg/USCODE-2011-title10/html/USCODE-2011-title10-subtitleA-partI-chap2-sec118.htm*, accessed February 2, 2017.

12. "Risk," Businessdictionary.com, available from *www.businessdictionary.com/definition/risk.html*, accessed April 25, 2017.

13. 10 U.S.C. § 118(c) (2014). Assessment or description of the "nature and magnitude" of risk have been staple features of Title 10 language since the 2001 *Quadrennial Defense Review* (QDR).

14. Mazarr, "Rethinking Risk in Defense."

15. This insight emerged in an interview with working-level members of the Joint Staff via video teleconference, September 22, 2016.

16. *ISO 31000 - Risk Management: Principles and guidelines*, International Organization for Standardization, 2009, available from *https://www.iso.org/iso-31000-risk-management.html*, accessed April 23, 2017. The ISO (International Organization for Standardization) is an independent, non-governmental membership

organization and the world's largest developer of voluntary International Standards. ISO describes *Risk Management* as the "development of a clear understanding of the risks that are important to the enterprise and managing them as the organization evolves and the operating environment (physical, environmental, financial and social) changes through time."

17. Chairman of the Joint Chiefs of Staff (CJCS), Chairman of the Joint Chiefs of Staff Manual (CJCSM) 3105.01, *Joint Risk Analysis*, Washington, DC: U.S. Department of Defense, October 14, 2016, pp. B5-B6, available from *www.jcs.mil/Library/*, accessed February 2, 2017.

18. The six areas include: the nature, clarity, and origin of defense challenges (hazards and demands) and their relationship to current U.S./partner conventions, priorities, and plans; the residual or hidden hazard or risk impacting defense challenges and prior U.S./partner approaches to mitigating, accepting, transferring, or avoiding it; the character, complexity, rate of change, and endurance of defense challenges and perceived U.S./partner competency, anticipation, adaptability, depth, and resilience to account for them; the scope, scale, and diversity of defense challenges and presumed U.S./partner capacity to absorb their attendant requirements; the spatial and temporal sequencing of the defense challenges matched to presumed U.S./partner responsiveness, reach, and flexibility of existing or assumed capabilities; and finally, overall judgment on existing U.S./partner defense leverage vis-à-vis the defense challenges, as well as identification of available opportunities that may generate distinct advantages for the United States and its partners.

19. CJCS, CJCSM 3105.01.

20. As it related to "gray zone" challenges last year, the study team opted to "describe" vice "define" these terms. In the study team's view, hard definitions can rapidly be overcome and are vulnerable to being rapidly overcome by events in the contemporary environment. For a view of how last year's study team handled this, see Nathan Freier, proj. dir., Charles R. Burnett, William J. Cain, Jr., Christopher D. Compton, Sean M. Hankard, Robert S. Hume, Gary R. Kramlich II, J. Matthew Lissner, Tobin A. Magsig, Daniel E. Mouton, Michael S. Muztafago, James M. Schultze, John F. Troxell, and Dennis G. Wille, cont. auths., *Outplayed: Regaining Strategic Initiative in the Gray Zone*, Carlisle, PA: Strategic Studies Institute, U.S. Army War College, 2016, available from *ssi.armywarcollege.edu/pubs/display.cfm?pubID=1325*, accessed May 3, 2017.

21. Nathan S. Lowrey, *The Chairmanship of the Joint Chiefs of Staff 1949-2016*, Washington, DC: The Joint History Office, Office of the Chairman of the Joint Chiefs of Staff, 2016, p. 347.

22. 10 U.S.C. § 118(a)(2)(C) (2011), available from *https://www.gpo.gov/fdsys/pkg/USCODE-2011-title10/html/USCODE-2011-title10-subtitleA-partI-chap2-sec118.htm*, accessed February 2, 2017.

II. STUDY METHODOLOGY

In July 2016, the United States Army War College (USAWC) initiated this study on enterprise-level risk and risk assessment with the support and sponsorship of the U.S. Army's Strategic Plans and Policy Directorate; the Joint Staff, J5 (Strategy and Policy Branch); the Office of the Deputy Secretary of Defense for Strategy and Force Development; and the Army Study Program Management Office. In support of priorities outlined in the memorandum, "Fiscal Year 2017 Army Study Planning Guidance," the USAWC assembled a study team of four faculty, eight students, and one outside policy professional to examine how the Department of Defense (DoD) risk conventions comport with a posited set of enduring defense objectives, current and future defense-relevant hazards threatening their security, and the military demands those hazards are prone to generate.[1] In the end, the study sought to offer where appropriate new perspectives on how DoD might describe, identify, assess, and communicate **strategic** and **military risk** in more effective and widely consumable ways.

This study is intended to provide an independent look at the key factors associated with and affecting enterprise-level **strategic** and **military risk** judgments and deliver additive findings and recommendations to the existing body of DoD's knowledge and work on the subject. It offers conclusions on how the defense enterprise might employ a common, cogent, and adaptable risk currency from risk identification through risk communication in order to better inform strategic decision-making by DoD senior leadership. Toward these ends, the study effort proceeded in four phases.

This study employed a four-phased approach:
- *Phase I: Develop preliminary insights*
- *Phase II: Refine and test insights*
- *Phase III: Record and report findings*
- *Phase IV: Socialize results*

In Phase I (Develop Preliminary Insights, July-October 2016), the USAWC study team sharpened the research focus, developed early insights, and conducted preliminary literature reviews. Most prominently, the latter included four individual surveys of literature looking at how various defense and non-defense parties defined risk and employed risk-based decision-making at the enterprise-level. These surveys examined risk processes and judgments in the private or commercial sector, from the perspective of individual U.S. service components (Army, Navy, Air Force, and Marine Corps), from the U.S. joint military perspective (both in the Pentagon and combatant commands), and finally, from the standpoint of U.S. Government senior leadership operating across the national security sector (including, but not limited to, DoD). Additionally, the USAWC study team collected and derived insights from a questionnaire that among other topics asked respondents to identify the top five potential U.S. "surge" demands defense senior leadership should anticipate between 2017 and 2027. This information was essential for the team identifying where DoD might anticipate "looking for risk" from now into the mid-term future.

The USAWC study benefited from early engagement with its expert working group (EWG) during Phase I. The first of three planned EWG sessions occurred in July 2016 — well before the final consolidation of the USAWC study team. As was the case last year with *Outplayed: Regaining Strategic Initiative in the Gray Zone*, the EWG represented a cross-section of meaningful voices from the broadest possible defense and military communities of interest.[2] EWG membership included representatives of the joint and service staffs, the Office of the Secretary of Defense (OSD), think tanks, private industry, and joint professional military education.

Phase II (Refine and Test Insights, November 2016-March 2017) opened with the second of three EWGs and included the third and final EWG deliberations in January 2017. Additionally, Phase II included significant periods of external engagement and research. During Phase II, members of the USAWC study team met personally or via video teleconference with representatives of three regional combatant commands and one functional combatant command (U.S. Central Command [USCENTCOM], U.S. Pacific Command [USPACOM], U.S. Northern Command [USNORTHCOM], and U.S. Special Operations Command [USSOCOM]); and one sub-unified joint command, U.S. Forces, Japan (USFJ). Members of the team also met with senior- and working-level representatives of two U.S. intelligence organizations (Defense Intelligence Agency [DIA] and the National Intelligence Council). Additionally, representatives of a second functional combatant command, U.S. Strategic Command (USSTRATCOM), submitted written responses and the study team reviewed the answers to those targeted research questions.

In addition to the combatant commands, the USAWC study team consulted with representatives of two regional service component commands (U.S. Army Pacific [USARPAC] and Pacific Fleet [PACFLT]), as well as engaged in roundtable discussions with the American Enterprise Institute, the Center for Strategic and International Studies (CSIS), the RAND Corporation, and the Institute for the Study of War.

During Phase III (Record and Report Findings, March-April 2017), the USAWC study team vetted the report's findings with its senior review group (SRG). The SRG offered final thoughts on the course, conduct, and conclusions of the work prior to final preparation of the effort's formal report. Naturally, Phase III included substantial report writing as well throughout. Phase III closed with a final briefing to the study's sponsors in April 2017 and submission of the final draft report to the USAWC Press for editing and publication.

Finally, with submission of the report to the USAWC Press, Phase IV (Socialize Results, May-August 2017) commenced with broad virtual and in-person socialization of the report's findings and recommendations. As of publication, Phase IV remains underway. Major events in Phase IV to date included a series of Washington-based "deskside" briefings to key stakeholders, a teleconference with the consulting universe associated with the Joint Staff, J-39 (Joint Multi-Layer Assessments Branch), as well as a formal rollout event at CSIS.

Finally, the study team would like to offer one last important concluding thought on the study methodology. Throughout, the team was fortunate to have the support of both its EWG and SRG. Without their insights, this study would not be as complete or fulsome as the team would have desired. Further, as was noted in the acknowledgments, this study represents the collective wisdom of all with whom the USAWC study team engaged. As in the case of the EWG and SRG, the report would not have been possible without their contributions. However, the study team would again like to reiterate that participation or contributions of all outside of the immediate USAWC study team does not imply their endorsement of the final product.

ENDNOTES – SECTION II

1. Department of the Army, "Fiscal Year 2017 Army Study Planning Guidance," Memorandum, Washington, DC: U.S. Department of Defense, March 2, 2016.

2. Nathan Freier, proj. dir., Charles R. Burnett, William J. Cain, Jr., Christopher D. Compton, Sean M. Hankard, Robert S. Hume, Gary R. Kramlich II, J. Matthew Lissner, Tobin A. Magsig, Daniel E. Mouton, Michael S. Muztafago, James M. Schultze, John F. Troxell, and Dennis G. Wille, cont. auths., *Outplayed: Regaining Strategic Initiative in the Gray Zone,* Carlisle, PA: Strategic Studies Institute, U.S. Army War College, 2016, available from *ssi.armywarcollege.edu/pubs/display.cfm?pubID=1325,* accessed May 3, 2017.

DESCRIBING RISK

III. THE LOGIC OF POST-PRIMACY RISK: CURRENT CONVENTIONS AND NEW TERMS OF REFERENCE

Risk is the most important dialogue there is [in the Department of Defense (DoD)]. Either you can [achieve objectives] or you can't.[1]

The concepts of risk and risk assessment in defense and military strategy and planning are by no means new to senior DoD leadership. There is to be sure a current risk convention or rubric that some within DoD adhere to, with the Joint Staff being the principal representative in this regard. The subjects of risk and risk assessment, however, remain areas of considerable disagreement or—perhaps better put—broad variance in corporate understanding and professional interpretation. In the end, the extent to which current convention truly establishes a common, enterprise-wide risk currency remains in doubt.

This is especially worrisome in light of the imperative to adapt to post-primacy circumstances. While the United States may still be the most important international actor in the state system, it can no longer count on the unassailable position of dominance, supremacy, or pre-eminence it enjoyed for the 20-plus years after the fall of the Soviet Union. Recognition of post-primacy is not a defeatist perspective. It is a wakeup call.[2]

The concept of post-primacy (explained in great detail in Section IV) is the basic recognition that global security affairs are much more competitive now than at any other time since the Cold War. Moreover, as such, the United States can no longer rely on unsophisticated combinations of raw political, economic, and military power as well as the latent attraction of example to force outcomes in its favor. The study team concluded and found wide recognition that more nimble and adaptable approaches to strategy and risk assessment are essential to regaining initiative and advantage within this hyper-competitive strategic environment.

[I]n the next 10 years, I expect the risk of interstate conflict in East Asia to rise, the vulnerability of our platforms and basing to increase, our technology edge to erode, instability to persist in the Middle East, and threats posed by violent extremist organizations to endure. Nearly any future conflict will occur on a much faster pace and on a more technically challenging battlefield.[3]

This report encourages senior DoD leaders to adapt their risk perspectives to the demands of a less ordered and more contested post-primacy strategic landscape. In lieu of mathematically rigorous tactically-informed risk assessment formats, it seeks to narrow the gaps between competing risk perspectives resident among different DoD entities and key defense-interested stakeholder communities with a more qualitative risk dialogue occurring at the most senior levels of DoD. There are a number of thoughtful voices on the subject of risk and risk assessment across DoD; this report endeavors to identify, synthesize, and refine their insights with those of the study team, its expert working group (EWG), and its senior review group (SRG).

CURRENT RISK CONVENTION

Over the course of 9 months, the U.S. Army War College (USAWC) study team found a great deal of past and current risk activity within DoD, most prominently the classified

"Chairman's Risk Assessment" (CRA) and the recently published Chairman of the Joint Chiefs of Staff Manual (CJCSM) 3105.01, *Joint Risk Analysis*.[4] There are also, of course, myriad standard visuals explaining where and how risk, and risk assessment, fit in the process of enterprise-level defense strategy development. Note, for example, Figure III-1 where risk is shown as an abstract imbalance between ends, ways, and means.

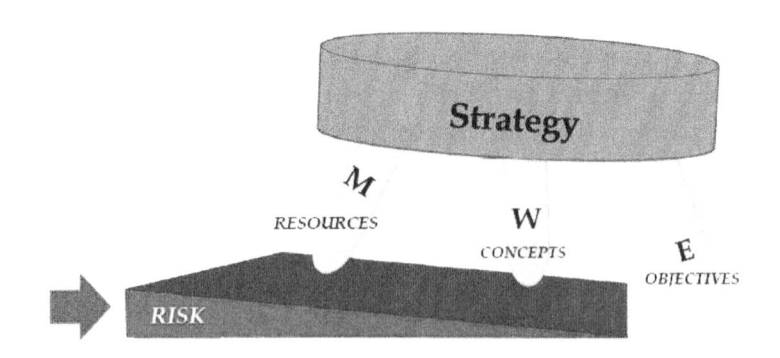

Figure III-1. Ends, Ways, Means, and Risk of the "Strategy Stool."[5]

While all of the aforementioned informed this study's findings and recommendations, it became abundantly clear through the course of the research effort that risk perspectives are not yet sufficiently integrated across civilian and military staffs, service components, and combatant commands. In short, there is no single, broad, consensus understanding—or concept—of exactly what constitutes risk in the context of the post-primacy environment and the major defense decisions and choices inevitably associated with it.

The CRA, for example, occurs on an annual basis. It is the product of bottom-up risk assessments percolating into the Joint Staff from regional and functional combatant commands, defense agencies, and military services. These insights are aggregated into a combined set of risk judgments under the CJCS' signature. The most significant or impactful among those judgments are forwarded to the Secretary of Defense and, by law, require formal risk mitigation plans.[6]

The most common critique of the CRA process is its inherent near-term focus. While it certainly attempts to project future risk, it likely does so as a linear extrapolation of the known hazards against which DoD already has well-established concepts and plans. An argument can also be made that the CRA is not articulated in a "common risk currency" that is widely accepted across various DoD risk consumers, nor does it account for higher corporate-level judgments on whether or not DoD has the environment and the enterprise-level azimuth right.

The new CJCSM, *Joint Risk Analysis*, originated in the Joint Staff for the expressed purpose of "promot[ing] consistency across [the] Department of Defense and Joint Force risk-related processes."[7] This latter point is a noble and meaningful goal that this study also hopes to contribute to with an alternative set of important perspectives. The CRA is rooted in near-term operational requirements of U.S. regional and functional combatant commands. The CJCSM, on the other hand, is more fundamentally grounded in the philosophy or concept of risk assessment. Both are important components of the current risk architecture but may not be dynamic or forward-looking enough, given the profound change afoot in the strategic environment.

This work proceeds first and foremost from a dynamic, near- to long-term, "objective/strategy vs. hazard" driven perspective. In short, it starts with "ends" expressed as objectives. It applies those objectives to context in order to identify the prospective "ways" (expressed as demands) to secure objectives. Finally, it suggests that risk assessment pace first against those demands essential to securing the most important among the identified objectives.

The study team determined that this approach was essential largely because the two aforementioned joint processes or initiatives do not yet constitute a unifying concept for all the risk-interested stakeholders. Further, neither is perceived by both the study team and the majority of those it engaged with to be sufficiently dynamic, forward-looking, or adaptive under contemporary conditions.

> **Quadrennial Defense Review (QDR) 2001, 9/11, and the Sudden Death of Convention**
>
> Published on June 22, 2001, the "Guidance and Terms of Reference" for the 2001 QDR appears naïve given the sudden change in defense trajectory that began 81 days later on September 11, 2001. As a charter for the 2001 QDR, it stated:
> *This review is based on the **premise** that, in combination with other instruments of national power, **the foundation of a peaceful world...rests on** the ability of the U.S. Armed Forces to maintain a **substantial margin of national military advantage relative to others**. The U.S. uses this advantage not to dominate others, but . . . to dissuade new functional or geographic military competitions from emerging and to manage them if they do* [emphasis in original, italics added].[8]

Thus, the USAWC study team found three clear vulnerabilities or shortcomings in current risk convention. First, it focuses too much on the most tangible near-term military threats (China, Russia, North Korea, etc.).[9] Second, it lacks a meaningful, crosscutting connection back to concrete defense objectives. It is, in a word, excessively "threat-based" in the most classic sense.[10] Moreover, it has finally proven to be an insufficient catalyst for essential post-primacy defense innovation and adaptation.

In short, while defense strategy and capabilities naturally favor known knowns—like traditional threats from China, Russia, Iran, North Korea, and myriad Islamic extremist groups—strategy development, risk identification, and risk assessment in reality should employ a wider, more imaginative perspective. As the velocity and vectors of consequential defense challenges increase geometrically, the utility of past defense and military problem-solving convention will inevitably collapse. Paraphrasing a senior Joint Staff officer charged with strategy development and risk assessment, the current system does not reward risk-based innovation.[11]

THREE COMPETING RISK PERSPECTIVES

The three shortcomings or vulnerabilities outlined previously trace their roots to the absence of a common (or commonly accepted) DoD risk concept. A commonly acknowledged risk concept is an essential component to designing coherent enterprise-level strategic direction.[12] For DoD, risk identification and assessment occur at different (vertical) levels of analysis and across varying (horizontal) time dimensions. The study team found that the extent to which these considerations are linked effectively is a point of considerable debate.

Further, the combination of static strategy development, strategic planning, and risk assessment processes with a hyper-dynamic post-primacy decision-making environment exacerbates the aforementioned shortcomings as well. Indeed, according to one veteran allied strategist, strategy and plans are still fundamentally based on "stability." In short, strategy and plans are made in a sterile vacuum—unperturbed by persistent real-world interventions. However, they are always executed or advanced in the more fluid, turbulent, and dynamic reality of real-world uncertainty.[13]

This condition is on constant display today. The strategic and operational environments are in persistent flux while the "best laid plans" are made (and often interrupted by reality) in the absence of a cogent risk concept that accounts for that dynamism. This study endeavors to provide a reasoned perspective on what a common post-primacy risk concept might look like in defense strategy and planning over the next decade.

[A]ll strategy requires stress testing. After all, even the most exquisite plans engender hazards. Therefore, identification of the vulnerabilities exposed by a chosen strategy's interactions with prospective rivals and rival circumstances requires thorough and deliberate risk assessment.[14]

The USAWC study team found three separate broad interpretations of risk or risk-focus within corporate DoD. The first is an excessively abstract conception of near-term strategic—almost geopolitical—risk. The second operational-level risk focuses on tangible near-term hazards and the plans associated with addressing them. Finally, there are risk perceptions and judgments of, on the one hand, the services who are responsible for manning, training, and equipping capable forces and, on the other hand, Joint theater leadership responsible for integrating those forces into their plans and competently employing them.

The first reflects the primary interest of senior civilian leaders at the top of DoD. Here, risk generally concerns DoD's ability to meet its broad global responsibilities given adopted strategies, plans, concepts, and capabilities. In short, currently the Department's corporate leadership sees itself as principally responsible for assessment of and judgments on what U.S. law and common DoD convention would identify as **strategic risk;** which, alternatively, is what current Joint Staff convention defines as:

> [T]he potential impact upon the United States—including U.S. populations, territory, civil society, critical infrastructure, and interests—of current and contingency events given their estimated consequences and probabilities.[15]

If that definition appears unsatisfying, given the explicit absence of any connection to concrete strategic objectives, the study team agrees. Indeed, one highly-regarded, working-level Joint Force risk professional observed that **strategic risk**—by this definition—lacked meaningful advocacy in defense deliberations.[16] This may be attributable in some measure to this vague definition or interpretation. As of this printing, it appears Congress has intervened to aptly relabel **strategic risk** as "strategic military risk."[17] However, this study will continue to employ the former term, albeit in an adapted context.

Among DoD's most senior joint military leadership, risk is by definition more granular and visceral, focusing more on mission accomplishment—often related directly to theater war plans, as well as the near-, mid-, and long-term viability of the Joint Force as it is employed pursuing U.S. security objectives. These are the twin considerations of "risk-to-mission" and "risk-to-force" that together capture the topic of **military risk** in joint parlance. Again, according to current joint thinking, **military risk** is:

> [T]he estimated probability and consequence of the Joint Force's projected inability to achieve current or future military objectives (risk-to-mission), while providing and sustaining sufficient military resources (risk-to-force).[18]

The study team concluded that **military risk** was more straightforward, widely understood, and easily consumable. This is perhaps a product of military risk being clearly linked to concrete real world military objectives. In both the team's view and that of at least one experienced Joint Staff risk professional, what is missing from the vertical **military**-to-**strategic risk** relationship was a clear understanding of the "connective tissue" linking the two.[19] Thus, there is in effect dead space unaccounted for in enterprise-level deliberations between the strategic and military levels of analysis. As in the case of **strategic risk**, Congress appears to have stepped in and recently relabeled what has heretofore been referred as **military risk**, now labeling it operational risk. In order to avoid confusion, this report will continue to use the term **military risk** (albeit with an adapted interpretation), as DoD still employs the term operational risk to suggest "current" or "immediate" risk as it applies to war plans and near-term concepts of operation. A great deal will be said on all of this shortly.

Finally, among the service components and combatant commands, the dominant risk theme is near-term readiness or what might be called a decidedly "fight tonight" perspective. This view is encapsulated perfectly in the sage perspective of one senior service strategist who observed that there is no meaningful advocate for "future challenges" risk within the service departments.[20] In his view, the component commanders (numbered fleets, air forces, and armies) alongside their respective service chiefs have a decidedly **operational** or near-term risk perspective.

Their business is "readiness" and, by implication, readiness implies an ability to meet immediate operational demands. Thus, as in the case of senior Joint Force leadership in the Pentagon, Joint Force commanders and the service chiefs who provide them trained and ready forces are firmly embedded in the same **military risk** space described previously. Moreover, often that space is narrowly confined to near-term planning considerations of what the Pentagon calls **operational risk**. Consequently—along the horizontal, time-driven assessment of risk—near-term **operational risk** considerations often trump longer-term **future challenges** risk. This not only mortgages future readiness, it further leaves significant uncovered dead space along the horizontal axis that connects the two as well.

These various competing (and sometimes fundamentally incomplete) perspectives do not necessarily need to be in perfect harmony. Indeed, one veteran Joint Staff risk professional argued that there actually should be tension in the risk assessment system between the various stakeholders and, by implication, the various vertical and horizontal axes of risk assessment.[21]

The study team agrees. However, the study's findings and recommendations do attempt to deliberately remove unnecessary disharmony and tension. The team breaks down what are by definition complex post-primacy risk considerations and offers a finite set of actionable recommendations that will materially aid in pushing all stakeholders toward a common perspective or common currency on risk and risk assessment as they affect corporate defense decision-making. This is crucial given the environment's predisposition for disruptive change.

NEW RISK TERMS OF REFERENCE

Given the absence of cogent cross-DoD agreement on the concept of risk, as well as the various tensions and competing perspectives on various aspects of the subject, the study team found it essential to establish foundational terms of reference for its analysis. In particular, nine key concepts are referenced and used throughout this work. They bind the work with an intellectual consistency and drive the underlying logic that leads to the study's findings and recommendations.

Some of these concepts are common to the current defense lexicon but are nonetheless interpreted differently or substantially adapted to increase their value in post-primacy strategy development and risk assessment. These foundational concepts include:
- Enduring Defense Objectives;
- 10-Year Defense Hazards;
- Surge;
- 10-Year Surge Demands;
- Principal Risk Portfolio;
- Strategic Risk;
- Military Risk;
- Operational Risk; and finally,
- Future Challenges Risk.

The study presents these nine concepts in a logical sequence or hierarchy. This sequence demonstrates a rational and progressive relationship between each concept and provides for a seamless conceptual transition from a general description of foundational ideas to their specific application in post-primacy strategy development, strategic planning, and risk assessment. This building block approach for the terms of reference underwrites the requisite consistency of thought necessary for senior leadership to evaluate this study's findings and recommendations, debate them vigorously—testing their utility in light of contemporary strategic conditions—and finally, adopt them in some form as essential components of their risk assessment toolbox.

ENDURING DEFENSE OBJECTIVES

The first foundational concept is that of **Enduring Defense Objectives**.[22] By surveying post-Cold War U.S. defense and national security policy, and after extensive vetting by both the EWG and SRG, the study team identified and adopted six defense-specific national-level objectives.[23]

In the team's judgment, these six illustrative objectives represent a reasonable strategic foundation for future DoD planning and risk assessment. The objectives provide strategists, planners, and senior decision-makers with a common launch point for identification of the measurable intentions underlying strategy and strategic plans. Clear strategic objectives further provide subordinate organizations and commands with enduring targets for making value judgments, setting institutional priorities, and conducting strategic planning. The study team took some cues in this regard from an unpublished U.S. Special Operations Command (USSOCOM) "Risk Concept Paper" that argued in part, "Discussing risk meaningfully requires making clear the answer to the question: Risk to what? In all cases, the answer should be related to prioritized organizational objectives."[24]

In the team's view, the six enduring defense objectives could withstand changes in national-level political leadership and strategic circumstances. And, thus, they provide for a common universal set of defense responsibilities against which the post-primacy strategic environment, its hazards, and its opportunities can readily be evaluated in order to identify the most important near-, mid-, and long-term pacing defense demands and their associated priority. While discussed later in more detail, the six **enduring defense objectives** employed in this report are:

- Secure U.S. territory, people, infrastructure, and property against significant harm.
- Secure access to the global commons and strategic regions, markets, and resources.
- Meet foreign security obligations.
- Underwrite a stable, resilient, rules-based international order.
- Build and maintain a favorable and adaptive global security architecture.
- Create, preserve, and extend U.S. military advantage and options.

DEFENSE-RELEVANT HAZARDS

The second concept in the terms of reference is that of **10-Year Defense-Relevant Hazards**. This list of unfiltered contingency events is derived from survey responses from key stakeholders representing the intelligence, defense strategy and planning, and defense analysis communities. In part, the hazards were identified from responses to the pre-study survey question, "What do you perceive to be DoD's top 5 potential **surge** military demands between 2017-2027?"

The study team also contributed to the articulation of **hazards** with their own individual responses to the same survey question. What is most important to understand about the hazards is the fact that they are not point predictions about future events. They are instead illustrative, prospective contingency events that would likely generate enormous debate among senior national leadership and, at the same time, trigger the consideration of major U.S. military commitments. The study will consider the concept of **surge** by itself in the next few sections.

As in the case of all major components of this report, the hazards were vetted by the study's EWG, SRG, and in the course of desk side encounters and roundtables, the study team engaged with key defense stakeholders. These stakeholders included both American and foreign partner national security leaders and analysts.

In the end, the hazards are one waypoint *en route* toward a new concept for identifying and assessing post-primacy **strategic** and **military risk**. The study team structured its research effort and report to illustrate a thought-provoking case for that new strategic baseline. Perhaps most thought provoking about the illustrative hazards is the fact that they include but are not defined or dominated by DoD's current "4 plus 1" threat-based model.[25]

The report's consumers will discover that careful comparison of identified defense-relevant hazards and their perceived impact on the **enduring defense objectives**—as well as their ultimate categorization under the rubric of eight generic **surge** defense demands—is the first step in creating a coherent **principal risk portfolio**. The report later suggests that the portfolio is a useful tool for categorizing an adopted defense strategy's military demands. Additionally, those demands, and the portfolio as a whole, are important pacers for persistent risk identification and assessment.

Later, the study team discusses in much greater detail the relationship between 10-year **defense hazards** and 10-year **surge demands**. However, for now, suffice it to say that the former is an unfiltered appreciation and assessment of speculative contingency problems that would be of enormous concern to DoD as they proceed with strategy development. The latter, on the other hand, are general expressions of the character of military responses to the identified hazards.

SURGE AS A FUNCTION OF RISK AND RISK ASSESSMENT

As the study team opened its work, it set out to determine the principal points of stress against which it would focus the examination or targeting of post-primacy risk and risk assessment. The study team determined that the point of maximum stress for defense leadership fell into the category of **surge** of some description, and further that the concept of **surge** would be a centerpiece in what the team determined were among the most important issues for senior defense leadership to tackle in formal and informal risk assessments.

The term **surge** was popularized in the national security vernacular by the relatively rapid infusion of military forces into Iraq between 2006 and 2009. It has since been accepted to mean a "significant increase in the number of troops deployed to an area."[26] This study took a fundamentally different approach to the concept of **surge**. It proceeded less from the perspective of **surge** as a function of geometry, mathematics, or dimensions, and much more from the perspective of **surge** as it relates to the concepts of "fixation" or "preoccupation."

Thus, for the purposes of this study, the term **surge** and **surge demand** are used to mean contingency commitments of defense and military resources, energy, and/or attention at levels that dominate DoD's decision making, planning, and priorities for a majority of one calendar year or more.[27] In the end, the study team concluded that **surge demand** commonly and correctly drives defense risk assessment at both the **strategic** and **military** levels of analysis. However, **surge demand** in the context of high-end combined arms warfighting—while no doubt fulfilling the definition outlined earlier—is no longer sufficient by itself as a yardstick for post-primacy risk assessment.

Purposeful actors posing complex, unconventional, or hybrid challenges — often in a wildly distributed fashion, as well as wicked contextual threats — arising in the complete absence of strategic purpose will generate their own less traditional **surge demands**.[28] The defense enterprise would be well advised to adapt its risk assessment conventions accordingly.

SURGE DEMANDS

The study team found that specific (but still illustrative) identification of **surge demands** is the next logical step for defense and military leaders responsible for strategy development and risk assessment.[29] Arrival at a workable set of **surge demands** that best characterizes potential military requirements over the next decade is first, a product of a comparison of **enduring defense objectives** with the environment within which they are secured and advanced, and the strategy employed to contend with the environment's unique hazards.

This process yields bins of like-type defense demands. The study team determined that bins of demand like these should drive planning, concepts, and capabilities development, and subsequently, risk identification and assessment at both the **strategic** and **military** levels of analysis.

This report identifies a single dominant institutional demand — persistent (at speed) adaptation and eight additional contingency **surge demands**. Together, the study team believes that these nine total demands should remain focus points for DoD's strategy and plans over the next decade. In consultation with various risk stakeholders, the study team concluded that the first — persistent adaptation — should, regardless of exogenous contingency circumstances, be a principal driver of intellectual and material energy over the next decade.[30]

As Section V will make perfectly clear, DoD's contemporary decision-making environment is extremely volatile. Indeed, this study found in consultation with multiple stakeholders that the scale and velocity of change in strategic conditions is so great, and the imperative for persistent adaptation across joint domains is so urgent, that this one dominant surge demand must remain at the forefront of DoD's strategy and risk assessment through the next decade and beyond. This late conclusion in the study effort was pathbreaking, in that it married within the new risk assessment concept the likelihood that persistent adaptation would likely occur both parallel to, and as a result of, the process of learning associated with contingency military demands.

In addition to persistent adaptation, eight additional contingency surge demands emerged from a comparison of objectives, illustrative hazards, and the study team's interpretation of the dominant military missions with the greatest potential to surface over the next decade. They include:
- Strategic Deterrence and Defense;
- Gray Zone/Counter-Gray Zone;
- Access/Anti-Access;
- Influence/Counter-Influence;
- Distributed Security;[31]
- Counter-Network;[32]

- Major Combat;[33] and
- Humanitarian Assistance and Consequence Management.[34]

A great deal more will be said about both adaptation and the eight contingency surge demands later in Section VI.

PRINCIPAL RISK PORTFOLIO

Filtering objectives through the environment and its hazards, identifying a cogent strategic approach to defending those objectives and, in the process, identifying key elements of the next decade's potential **surge demand** terminates for risk assessment purposes in identification of what this study calls DoD's **principal risk portfolio**. The portfolio is the conceptual location of the most important defense demands for the forthcoming decade.[35] These are identified in the strategy development process and persistently reviewed and assessed as strategic circumstances evolve. The surge demands are evaluated (and, by implication, prioritized) within the portfolio according to four key criteria—**importance**, **urgency**, **capability/capacity**, and perceived U.S. **agility**.[36] Naturally, final prioritization is negotiable based on circumstances, context, and senior-level judgment.

Importance implies judgments as to an individual demand's criticality to the defense or security of one or more at-risk **enduring defense objectives**. Employing the common risk language of "likelihood" and "consequence" as a reference, **importance** marries what current joint language calls "strength of interest" with the concept of measurable "consequences."[37]

In the abstract, **surge demands** are unsurprisingly considered more important to the extent they match up directly to defense or security of the highest priority or greatest number of defense objectives. In spite of a great deal of available data, this will most likely be an "instinct" call based on the best "crowd-sourced" debate and dialogue among defense and national security strategists and planners and the final judgment of the most senior defense and executive branch leadership.

Urgency is both an objective and subjective call on the extent and timing of required action. Urgent demands, for example, may require application of resources and capabilities now in order to: 1) actively meet specific demands immediately, or 2) to cover down on an obvious and/or dangerous vulnerability that may become active in the indeterminate future. At its core, **urgency** involves time-dependent judgments related to when senior leadership believe a particular demand will be either most operative or most vulnerable. Again employing some common risk language, **urgency** is the marriage of a hazard's "likelihood" with the velocity of its emergence, its rate of change or adaptation, and the perceived ability of DoD and partner defense establishments to meet or adapt to it.

Capability/capacity involve informed aggregate judgments on the degree to which the U.S. defense enterprise is already equipped and postured to meet identified **surge demands**. **Capability** implies material and conceptual readiness. **Capacity**, on the other hand, requires judgments on the extent of the anticipated demand in scope, scale, and duration matched with breadth and endurance of available U.S. and partner responses.

Finally, **agility** involves senior judgments on the degree to which DoD can flex to the unique requirements of a particular demand whether or not pre-existing **capability/ capacity** is deemed present and employable. Implicit in **agility** is the ability to adapt as well. Thus, it is not just about the ability to swing existing resources to new challenges but, in fact, it is about adapting or creating capabilities and concepts to meet unanticipated or under-anticipated demands.

STRATEGIC AND MILITARY RISK

The study team started its inquiry with two clear ideas in mind on the subject of describing risk at the **strategic** and **military** levels of analysis. These ideas were validated by the study's EWG and SRG. First, the team concluded (not unlike the previous year's "gray zone" work) that detailed definitions are vulnerable to being or becoming invalid via over-precision as soon as they are promulgated. As a consequence, and consistent with the team's belief in risk assessment more as a structured dialogue than a precise formula, it opted to "describe" vice "define" these concepts in order to allow for their interpretation and adaptation when applied by senior leadership to real world hazards and demands.[38]

In the end, the study team sides with RAND analyst Michael Mazarr, who artfully concluded that risk assessment is more about senior leader discourse than it is point solutions. This lends itself to a common understanding of the concepts of **strategic** and **military risk** vice an immutable doctrinal or dogmatic definition. In this regard, Mazarr observes:

> An effective risk process should force decision makers to talk about potential consequences in rigorous and nuanced terms, with the goal of informing and shaping their judgment. The risk assessments themselves are not the goal—they are only means to the broader objective of risk-informed decision-making.[39]

A second principle the study ascribes to on the subject of **strategic** and **military risk** is the simple narrative that there can be no risk without something first being at stake, as well as an obvious corollary to that concept: "you have to generate risk [in order] to assume [and assess] risk."[40] Mazarr is again instructive on this point when, in his recent War on the Rocks essay "Rethinking Risk in Defense," he observed, "In its simplest sense, the concept of risk refers to things that can go wrong in relation to something we value."[41]

Risk is not, therefore, just bad things that might occur. It is instead the prospect of hazards emerging in pursuit of a given set of objectives. And, the likelihood that those hazards will either lead to failure or unacceptable costs with respect to preferred outcomes. In this regard, risk involves twin judgments on two specific questions.

First, given a set of objectives, an adopted course of action, and allocated resources, is the purpose or object sought achievable? And, second, in light of the same foundational conditions, is the purpose or object sought worth the projected investment or will it be too costly in lives, money, material, political capital, and opportunities delayed or lost? This tracks with the findings of last year's gray zone report, *Outplayed: Regaining Strategic Initiative in the Gray Zone*, and its characterization of risk. That report found that:

All risk assessment involves informed judgments on the likelihood and consequences of failure that are associated with a strategy or some component of it. Risk arrives via manifest vectors. There is, for example, ample room to misjudge the character of principal threats, the extent of one's own limitations, or the scope and scale of the environment's most challenging obstacles to mission accomplishment.[42]

In order to cover the waterfront of potential descriptions, the study team began examining **strategic** and **military risk** through the lens of existing definitions or perspectives that are codified either in U.S. law or in common DoD practice and convention. For example, Title 10 U.S.C. § 113 requires the Secretary of Defense to—at a minimum—produce a *National Defense Strategy* (NDS) every 4 years that among other requirements provides:

A strategic framework . . . that guides how the Department will prioritize among the threats described in clause (ii) and the missions specified pursuant to clause (i) [and] **how the Department will allocate and mitigate the resulting risks** [emphasis added].[43]

Specific references to **strategic** and **military** risk, as well as the "nature and magnitude" thereof have been fixtures of U.S. defense legislation for nearly 2 decades as well.[44] Yet, neither **strategic** nor **military** risk has ever been defined or described by the legislature over that same time period. As previously discussed, the current National Defense Authorization Act (NDAA) modified Title 10, and in the process, characterized the concepts of **strategic** and **military** risk differently when describing the Chairman's responsibilities in strategy and risk assessment. It requires the Chairman to "Identify and define the military strategic [i.e., **strategic**] and operational [i.e., **military**] risks to United States interests and the military strategic and operational risks in executing the National Military Strategy [NMS]."[45]

As DoD continues to use **military** and **strategic** risk as terms of reference, this report will do so as well. The important point here is that whatever the levels of analysis are called, their definition will most likely remain in the hands of DoD and its leadership.

The Joint Staff defined both terms in their most recent 2016, CJCSM 3105.01, *Joint Risk Analysis*. They identify **strategic risk** as "the potential impact upon the United States . . . of current and contingency events given their estimated consequences and probabilities."[46] Whereas, **military risk** is "the estimated probability and consequences of the Joint Force's projected inability to achieve current or future military objectives . . . while providing and sustaining sufficient military resources."[47]

Given the logic outlined thus far, the USAWC study team opted for two broad descriptions of **strategic** and **military risk** that conform to the team's emerging perspective on the post-primacy environment and the risk-based strategic-choices likely to emerge from it. In broad terms, the study team's risk descriptions are consistent with the current Joint Staff definitions, the basic intent of U.S. Code, and the last definitions of the two terms promulgated by the Office of the Secretary of Defense (OSD) in the 2010 QDR. However, the team found its descriptions most consistent with the broad and adaptable definitions articulated in the latter.

In the 2010 QDR, the OSD argued that **strategic risk** captured DoD-level judgments on DoD's "ability to execute enduring defense objectives in the near-term, mid-term, and long-term."[48] In addition, it further suggested that **military risk** involved senior insights on "the ability of U.S. forces to adequately resource, execute, and sustain military operations in the near- to mid-term, and the mid- to longer-term."[49]

From these various points of departure and informed by last year's gray zone report, the team arrived at two alternative working descriptions of **strategic** and **military risk**. On strategic risk, specifically, the team was particularly taken with a contribution by Robert Haddick, an EWG member and a Visiting Senior Fellow at the Mitchell Institute for Aerospace Studies of the Air Force Association. Haddick described **strategic risk** this way:

> [Strategic risk] is . . . the chance of grossly misjudging the future operating environment such that the strategist and his forces are not prepared for a highly consequential security failure. . . . The strategy failure would occur when the strategist has not prepared for . . . events which his process and force planning failed to anticipate.[50]

With all of the various inputs in mind, this report's description of **strategic risk** also tracks closely with the risk description in 2016's USAWC report *Outplayed*.[51] Thus, in the context of this study, the report argues that **strategic risk** might be described as:

> The likelihood that DoD: 1) fails to adequately anticipate urgent and important surge demands in its principal risk portfolio, and therefore, 2) incurs "increased prospects for either drastic under-performance, [prohibitive cost] or outright failure" securing enduring defense objectives.[52]

Post-primacy **military risk**, on the other hand and according to the study team, is:

> Overall or mission-specific judgments on the likelihood of "failure or prohibitive cost" associated with securing enduring defense objectives through the employment of military force and/or forces in the demands captured in the principal risk portfolio.[53]

Key insights on both the **strategic** and **military** levels of analysis are important to highlight here. First, in simple terms, **strategic risk** is "top-down." As such, it is the principal purview of the Secretary of Defense, informed by the advice of his key civilian and military advisors. It represents the secretary's best judgment on the likelihood that DoD has failed to effectively identify, focus, and/or define the **principal risk portfolio** and its most important demands. It is in a word, an assessment of the prospect for errors of omission at the highest levels of DoD.

In essence, **strategic risk** involves informed judgments on the likelihood that senior defense leaders have collectively pointed DoD in the wrong direction. Therefore, calculation of **strategic risk** requires the courage of honest self-reflection at the highest levels of DoD. Of the two levels of risk analysis, **strategic risk** is the greatest source of potential "shock."[54] Thus, the short hand for failure in this regard entails inadequate enterprise-level "shock-proofing."

Military risk, on the other hand, is more "bottom-up" and lies principally in the CJCS' lane. However, it is also informed "top-down" by the risk insights of senior civilian leadership. Moreover, this report ultimately concludes that the Secretary, by virtue of his being in the chain of command, "owns" corporate risk at all levels of analysis.

Military risk assesses the likelihood that defense and military leadership fail to adequately account for and/or counter specific demands inside the **principal risk portfolio**. As opposed to **strategic risk**, it is an informed judgment of the prospects for gross errors of commission or the potential that, once identified, senior leadership commits energy and resources against specific defense demands in ways that either drastically increase cost or result in operational-level defeat or failure.

> *A difficult problem to overcome in implementing more effective risk practices arises from the fact that it requires the organization to identify . . . weakness and underperformance. There is a natural resistance to undertaking a revision of procedures that will routinely identify these problems.*[55]

OPERATIONAL AND FUTURE CHALLENGES RISK

If **strategic** and **military risk** represent a vertical risk relationship in the defense context—one judgment on the adequacy of DoD's overall azimuth and the second on the ability of DoD to take on discrete military challenges to secure at-risk objectives—then **operational** and **future challenges risk** represent the most important horizontal risk relationship. In order to satisfy the legislative requirement to address risk in DoD's 2001 QDR, Donald Rumsfeld and the Bush administration ushered in a four-point risk assessment framework: **operational risk**, **future challenges risk**, force management risk, and institutional risk.[56]

From the outset, the study team determined that this report would focus primarily on risk related to defending or securing DoD's enduring defense objectives—or the ability of DoD to meet its external demands within acceptable cost. These are the general considerations that DoD (or, more specifically, the Joint Staff) might refer to as "risk-to-mission" and "risk-to-force."[57] The team concluded that the study would specifically focus here in order to narrow the report's findings and recommendations to those most likely to affect DoD's overall strategic direction.

While insights on the adequacy and overall health of specific components of Joint Force structure ("force management risk") or DoD's organization and business practices ("institutional risk") are important considerations, this study consciously targets higher order risk and its impact on the strategic direction and missioning of DoD and its constituent components, forces, agencies, and activities. Thus, this study examines the vertical risk continuum existing between the **strategic** and **military** levels of analysis, as well as the horizontal risk continuum that runs from current **operational risk** forward toward and through **future challenges risk**.[58]

In contemporary military thought, the former **operational risk** involves informed senior leader judgments on "the current force's ability to attain current military objectives," whereas, the latter **future challenges risk** considers "the future forces ability to achieve future mission objectives over the near and mid-term."[59] The study team agrees with these perspectives with some minor adaptation.

In short, this study argues that **operational risk** involves judgments on the current force's ability to meet prioritized surge defense demands and secure at-risk enduring defense objectives over the near-term (0-5 years). In addition, **future challenges risk** involves an identical assessment over the mid- to long-term (6-10 years). By definition, **future challenges risk** will be more dynamic in nature than will **operational risk**—as the study has concluded that both urgent and important enduring defense objectives, as well as contingency surge demands will shift in priority given changes in context. At both the **strategic** and **military** levels of analysis, the study team concluded that the dead space between **operational risk** and **future challenges risk**, as well as judgments on the character and rate of change in the environment and its hazards are among the most important sources of enterprise-level disruption and hazard (see Figure III-2).

Two Key Risk Axes: Military/Strategic and Operational/Future Challenges

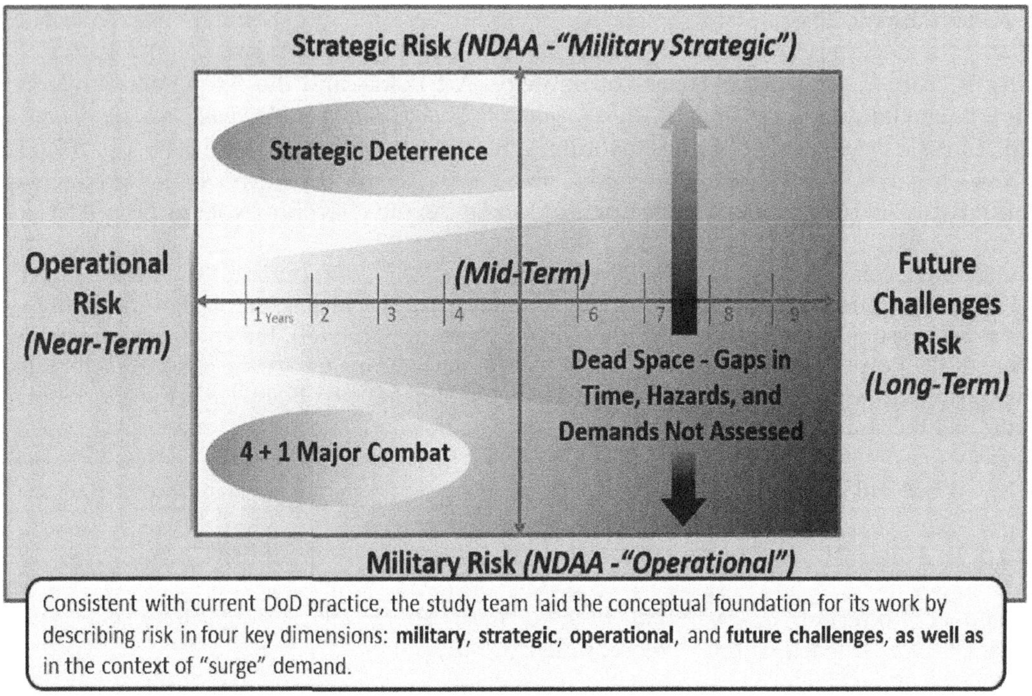

Figure III-2. Two Key Axes of Risk Assessment.

In Section IV, the study team explores the enduring defense objectives and their post-primacy evolution in significant detail. And, immediately thereafter in Section V, the report identifies the key characteristics and associated defense implications of DoD's post-primacy decision-making environment. Both are essential first steps in describing DoD's new risk concept.

ENDNOTES – SECTION III

1. This quote came from a senior Joint Staff officer in Washington, DC, April 11, 2017.

2. The concept of "post-primacy" was virtually unchallenged in individual interviews, roundtables, and expert working group (EWG) sessions. The study team however did encounter some unease with the term "post-primacy" from the senior review group (SRG). After consideration, the team decided to retain the concept as a central idea of the report and its findings. There was a consensus belief that the term reflected a new competitive reality and that it would serve as an important warning to DoD's senior leadership on the need for new perspectives on strategy and risk.

3. Martin E. Dempsey, "Chairman's Assessment of the Quadrennial Defense Review," in Department of Defense (DoD), *Quadrennial Defense Review 2014*, Washington, DC: U.S. Department of Defense, March 4, 2014, p. 61, available from *archive.defense.gov/pubs/2014_Quadrennial_Defense_Review.pdf*, accessed May 3, 2017.

4. For a description of the Chairman's Risk Assessment (CRA), see Chairman of the Joint Chiefs of Staff (CJCS), Chairman of the Joint Chiefs of Staff Instruction (CJCSI) 3100.01C, *Joint Strategic Planning System*, November 20, 2015, p. B-4, available from *www.jcs.mil/Library/CJCS-Instructions/*, accessed April 23, 2017; CJCS, Chairman of the Joint Chiefs of Staff Manual (CJCSM) 3105.01, *Joint Risk Analysis*, Washington, DC: U.S. Department of Defense, October 14, 2016, pp. A1-A4, available from *www.jcs.mil/Library/CJCS-Manuals/*, accessed February 2, 2017.

5. Harry R. Yarger, "Toward a Theory of Strategy: Art Lykke and the Army War College Strategy Model," in J. Boone Bartholomees, Jr., ed., *U.S. Army War College Guide to National Security Policy and Strategy*, 2nd ed., Carlisle, PA: Strategic Studies Institute, U.S. Army War College, June 2006, pp. 107-113. Figure adapted from Yarger, p. 110. The Strategy Model, also known as the "Lykke Model," was developed by a former Army War College (USAWC) professor, Art Lykke. As the reference explains on p. 110:

Art Lykke gave coherent form to a theory of strategy with his articulation of the three-legged stool model of strategy which illustrated that strategy = ends + ways + means, and if these were not in balance, the assumption of greater risk. In the Lykke proposition (model), the ends are 'objectives,' the ways are the 'concepts' for accomplishing the objectives, and the means are the 'resources' for supporting the concepts. The stool tilts if the three legs are not kept in balance. If any leg is too short, the risk is too great and the strategy falls over.

6. CJCS, CJCSM 3105.01, pp. A1-A4.

7. *Ibid.*, p. 1.

8. Donald H. Rumsfeld, *Guidance and Terms of Reference for the 2001 Quadrennial Defense Review*, Washington, DC: U.S. Department of Defense, June 22, 2001, p. 1.

9. A repeated theme throughout interactions with defense and defense-interested stakeholders found that there was concern that the future or future challenges were not adequately represented in DoD's contemporary risk conventions.

10. David Strachan-Morris, "Threat and Risk: What is the Difference and Why does it Matter?" *Intelligence and National Security*, Vol. 27, No. 2, April 27, 2012, pp. 175-180, accessed April 4, 2017.

11. This insight emerged from consultation with a senior Joint Staff officer in Washington, DC, April 11, 2017.

12. CJCS, CJCSM 3105.01, p. A-4.

13. Interview with a senior allied strategist in Washington, DC, February 2, 2017.

14. Nathan Freier, proj. dir., Charles R. Burnett, William J. Cain, Jr., Christopher D. Compton, Sean M. Hankard, Robert S. Hume, Gary R. Kramlich II, J. Matthew Lissner, Tobin A. Magsig, Daniel E. Mouton, Michael S. Muztafago, James M. Schultze, John F. Troxell, and Dennis G. Wille, cont. auths., *Outplayed: Regaining Strategic Initiative in the Gray Zone*, Carlisle, PA: Strategic Studies Institute, U.S. Army War College, 2016, p. 25, available from *ssi.armywarcollege.edu/pubs/display.cfm?pubID=1325*, accessed May 3, 2017.

15. CJCS, CJCSM 3105.01, p. C-4.

16. Roundtable interview with working-level Joint Staff strategists via video teleconference, September 22, 2016.

17. S. 2943, *National Defense Authorization Act for Fiscal Year 2017*, Public Law No: 114-328, 114th Cong., 2nd sess., December 23, 2016, § 943 (a)(1)(D)(3), p. 371, available from *https://www.congress.gov/bill/114th-congress/senate-bill/2943/text*, accessed May 3, 2017.

18. CJCS, CJCSM 3105.01, p. C-8.

19. Roundtable interview with recognized national security policy analysts, February 16, 2017.

20. Interview with a senior U.S. military service strategist via video teleconference, September 21, 2017.

21. *Ibid.*

22. See Dempsey, p. 60. The description of enduring defense interests track with or are equivalent to the "six national security interests" outlined by the CJCS in his public risk assessment of the *Quadrennial Defense Review* (QDR) 2014.

23. These broad categories were arrived at after (1) reviewing key strategic guidance documents - particularly those published after 1990 including (but not limited to) the *National Security Strategy*, QDR Reports, *National Defense Strategy* (NDS), and *National Military Strategy* (NMS); (2) considering the idea of "enduring" in context of identifying core objectives that have not substantially changed over the last 25+ years and are likely to remain given current and future anticipated world trends; and (3) after vigorous debate with our EWGs and validation by our SRG. While the study team recognizes that one may question whether these objectives will or will not, in fact, endure, we are confident that the six categories chosen represent broad consensus and wide approval among an extended field of national security experts and practitioners.

24. U.S. Special Operations Command (USSOCOM), "Risk Concept Paper," unpublished staff paper provided to the study team on a visit to USSOCOM headquarters at MacDill Air Force Base, FL, January 17, 2017, p. 1.

25. This point was made clear in roundtable consultation with working-level staff officers from the Office of the Secretary of Defense (OSD) in Washington, DC, April 11, 2017. For reference to the "4 plus 1," see Jim Garamone, "Dunford Details Implications of Today's Threats on Tomorrow's Strategy," DoD News, August 23, 2016, available from *https://www.defense.gov/News/Article/Article/923685/dunford-details-implications-of-todays-threats-on-tomorrows-strategy/*, accessed April 23, 2017. In remarks to National Defense University Students, General (GEN) Dunford observed, "We use those four state actors and one nonstate actor . . . to get an appreciation for where is the force relative to where it needs to be." This point was made clear in roundtable consultation with working-level staff officers from the OSD in Washington, DC, April 11, 2017.

26. "surge," Dictionary.com Unabridged, n.d., available from *www.dictionary.com/browse/surge*, accessed February 8, 2017.

27. This definition comes from the pre-study survey circulated to various defense-interested stakeholders.

28. Nathan Freier, "Known Unknowns: Unconventional 'Strategic Shocks' in Defense Strategy Development," *PKSOI Papers*, Carlisle, PA: Strategic Studies Institute, U.S. Army War College, 2008, p 16.

29. See Dempsey, pp. 60-61. The description of "10-Year Surge Demands" track or are equivalent to the 12 priority missions outlined by the CJCS in his public risk assessment of QDR 2014.

30. The study team concluded after consultations with a number of strategy and risk stakeholders that this dominant "surge demand" was in fact an overarching imperative for risk assessment specifically.

31. This demand and its description were adopted from Nathan Freier, proj. dir., David Berteau, prog. dir., Stephanie Sanok, Jacquelyn Guy, Curtis Buzzard, Errol Laumann, Steven Nicolucci, J.P. Pellegrino, Sam Eaton, and Megan Loney, cont. auths., *Beyond the Last War: Balancing Ground Forces and Future Challenges Risk in USCENTCOM and USPACOM*, Washington, DC: Center for Strategic and International Studies, 2013, p. 60.

32. This demand and its description were adopted from Nathan Freier, pri. auth., Daniel Bilko, Matthew Driscoll, Akhil Iyer, Walter Rugen, Terrence Smith, Matthew Trollinger, cont. auths., Maren Leed, proj. dir., *U.S. Ground Force Capabilities Through 2020*, Washington, DC: Center for Strategic and International Studies, October 2011, p. 3.

33. Freier *et al.*, *Beyond the Last War*, p. 90.

34. *Ibid.*, p. 80.

35. Freier, "Known Unknowns," p. 16.

36. These four criteria evolved throughout the course of the study. The team arrived at the first two early in the process. The last two emerged from significant internal deliberation and debate among study team members.

37. CJCS, CJCSM 3105.01, pp. GL-4, B-3, C-7.

38. Freier *et al.*, *Outplayed*, pp. 4-5.

39. Michael J. Mazarr, "Fixes for Risk Assessment in Defense," War on the Rocks, April 22, 2015, available from *https://warontherocks.com/2015/04/fixes-for-risk-assessment-in-defense/*, accessed February 9, 2017.

40. The quoted insight here emerged from an interview with a senior allied officer in the U.S. Pacific Command (USPACOM) Area of Responsibility (AoR), March 6, 2017.

41. Michael J. Mazarr, "Rethinking Risk in Defense," War on the Rocks, April 13, 2015, available from *https://warontherocks.com/2015/04/rethinking-risk-in-defense/?singlepage=1*, accessed February 9, 2017.

42. Freier *et al.*, *Outplayed*, p. 25.

43. See *Secretary of Defense*, 10 U.S.C. § 113(g)(1)(B)(iii) (2017), available from *uscode.house.gov/view.xhtml?req=granuleid:USC-prelim-title10-section113&num=0&edition=prelim*, accessed May 3, 2017.

44. The most recent references in this regard can be found in CJCS, CJCSM 3105.01, p. A-3.

45. *Chairman: functions*, 10 U.S.C. § 153(b)(2)(B)(ii) (2017), available from *uscode.house.gov/view.xhtml?req=granuleid:USC-prelim-title10-section153&num=0&edition=prelim*, accessed May 3, 2017.

46. CJCS, CJCSM 3105.01, pp. C-3-C-4, C-8.

47. *Ibid.*

48. DoD, *Quadrennial Defense Review 2010*, Washington, DC: U.S. Department of Defense, February 2010, p. iv.

49. *Ibid.*

50. Robert Haddick, Survey response delivered via email, October 18, 2017.

51. Freier *et al.*, *Outplayed*, p. 26.

52. See *Ibid.* The study team found that the description of risk included in last year's report *Outplayed* provided significant inspiration for this report's description of strategic risk.

53. DoD, *National Defense Strategy of the United States of America*, Washington, DC: U.S. Department of Defense, 2005, p. 11.

54. Freier, "Known Unknowns," p. 6.

55. USSOCOM, p. 5.

56. DoD, *Quadrennial Defense Review 2014*, pp. 57-58.

57. CJCS, CJCSM 3105.01, pp. C-8, C12-C13.

58. DoD, *National Defense Strategy 2008*, Washington, DC: U.S. Department of Defense, June 2008, p. 21.

59. *Ibid.*

IDENTIFYING RISK

IV. SECURING U.S. POSITION: SIX ENDURING DEFENSE OBJECTIVES

If the United States begins with a threat assessment before a conceptualization of interests . . . it risks reacting to a threat with major commitments and resources devoid of any rational linkage to the relative critical value of interests.[1]

ENDURING DEFENSE OBJECTIVES AS A CONCEPT

If both **strategic** and **military risk** judgments are informed calculations of the likelihood that the Department of Defense (DoD) and its constituent military forces are postured for the wrong world or—due to mischaracterization or miscalculation—hazard failure or unacceptable consequences securing core interests, then the study team found it reasonable to begin its analysis by identifying and vetting a universal set of enduring defense objectives. The team derived these postulated defense-specific goals from a review of 25 years of national security policy and defense strategy.[2] The objectives were finalized in consultation with the study's expert working group (EWG) and senior review group (SRG). In addition, they were thoroughly vetted during numerous roundtable engagements with important defense and defense-interested stakeholders.

While the team acknowledges that the world changes over time and the strategic environment against which the U.S. defense instrument is focused changes as well, the foundational review of U.S. national security and defense policy established precedents from which the team identified core objectives that, in some form, could reasonably be expected to endure and survive. Furthermore, these objectives would remain basically intact regardless of even drastic changes in strategic circumstances or the routine or extraordinary turnover of U.S. political leadership. The enduring defense objectives represent a common, foundational perspective on U.S. national interests as they relate to DoD and its central role in defending and advancing the same.

This study identified six enduring defense objectives as a result of an extensive survey of U.S. post-Cold War defense and security policy:

- *Secure U.S. territory, people, infrastructure, and property against significant harm.*

- *Secure access to the global commons and strategic regions, markets, and resources.*

- *Meet foreign security obligations.*

- *Underwrite a stable, resilient, rules-based international order.*

- *Build and maintain a favorable and adaptive global security architecture.*

- *Create, preserve, and extend U.S. military advantage and options.*

Further still, while the study team found that the United States might not necessarily persist as a static status quo power, the team's findings suggest that these objectives nonetheless would remain valid in general albeit in a different, adapted context. In the end, it is important to recall that the purpose of this study is not necessarily to pass judgment on current strategies or risk assessments, but instead the study offers senior defense leadership alternative ways of describing, identifying, assessing, and finally communicating **strategic** and **military risk**.

Collectively, the enduring defense objectives outlined here are an attempt to begin establishing a new strategic concept for the identification and evaluation of key defense-relevant hazards to national security interests and defense objectives. In the end, the study team and the broad cross-section of stakeholders with which it engaged believe that an objective-based vice threat-based risk assessment is the most appropriate approach for DoD and its constituent organizations.[3] Thus, identifying objectives like those described in the next section is a first step in more effective strategy development, risk identification, and risk assessment.

ENDURING OBJECTIVES FIRST

Often strategy development and risk assessment start with a gross appreciation of the strategic environment and then continue to the identification of objectives. This study proceeds from the foundational assumption that early appreciation of strategic objectives or ends subsequently applied to the strategic context within which the ends are pursued renders a clearer understanding of the most important defense demands and their vulnerabilities. As one senior leader in the U.S. Pacific Command (USPACOM) Area of Responsibility (AoR) stated, "without a defined goal, you can't even assess risk."[4] Thus, the study team suggests that enduring defense objectives like those to be discussed shortly might ultimately be used to: 1) develop a cogent defense strategy, 2) identify the likeliest surge demands associated with that strategy, and finally, 3) assess and manage the risk associated with DoD's actively meeting those demands.

Recall the study team's assertion in the introduction of this report: risk does not exist in a vacuum. In short, one cannot either identify or assess risk without first recognizing important national waypoints held in jeopardy by the strategic environment's most compelling hazards. Indeed, what commonly passes for risk in strategic deliberations is simply the raw expression of hazards or unfavorable developments that may emerge; often, all done in the absence of any meaningful evaluation of those hazards against either strategic objectives or intentions (ends) or the defense courses of action or demands adopted to secure them (ways).

The objectives outlined here are purposefully broad, as it was the judgment of the study team and its supporting EWG that their precise interpretation should by necessity be context dependent.[5] This is a reflection of the team's early recognition that context and accompanying defense priorities are likely to change significantly over time. Broad U.S. interests, on the other hand, will remain largely static. So too, therefore, should DoD's enduring defense objectives.

With major changes in the environment, DoD will naturally adapt to its new context. Nonetheless, the enduring defense objectives should remain a relatively stable set of adaptable touchstones for strategic decision-making among DoD's civilian and uniformed leadership. They should also be among the very first pacing considerations for focusing strategy development, strategic planning, and finally, the identification and assessment of **strategic** and **military risk**.

Thus, the objectives outlined in the next section provide valuable conceptual bins that successive Secretaries of Defense and Chairmen of the Joint Chiefs of Staff (CJCS) can fill with appropriate context and relevant detail in order to identify defense-relevant hazards as they emerge or persist.

SIX ENDURING DEFENSE OBJECTIVES

The study team identified the following as a contemporary set of foundational enduring defense objectives:
- Secure U.S. territory, people, infrastructure, and property against significant harm.
- Secure access to the global commons and strategic regions, markets, and resources.
- Meet foreign security obligations.
- Underwrite a stable, resilient, rules-based international order.
- Build and maintain a favorable and adaptive global security architecture.
- Create, preserve, and extend U.S. military advantage and options.

In most cases, these six objectives are a synthesis or adaptation of past, current, and projected U.S. defense policy.[6] There has been, after all, remarkable consistency in U.S. policy since the fall of the Soviet Union, regardless of which political party occupied the White House. The following provides a full description of each objective in its post-primacy context.

Secure U.S. Territory, People, Infrastructure, and Property against Significant Harm.

American senior leaders will be increasingly taxed to cut down or limit the vectors by which direct threats arrive to undermine the basic security of the United States, its people, territory, and holdings. Both consequential threats and effective responses are more sophisticated and diverse than at any time in U.S. history. From a **strategic** and **military risk** perspective, this first objective has historically been job one for DoD.[7] In the contemporary post-primacy environment, air and maritime sovereignty, defense of the physical approaches to American territory, counterterrorism, ballistic and cruise missile defense, and post-disaster security and relief are not the only defense roles in this regard.

The aforementioned and the significant harm they are focused against remain important components of defining and ultimately securing this particular objective. However, it would be fair to argue that the United States faces a range of fundamental hazards from across joint domains (including and increasingly most troubling—the cyber domain). Further, it faces new or growing challenges from and within the electromagnetic spectrum, on and from the bloodless battlefields of information and influence, and finally, from the leaderless forces of social disintegration and virtual mobilization and resistance.[8]

In the end, the purpose of this objective is captured succinctly in the 2009 *Quadrennial Roles and Missions Review Report* (QRM) and its description of "Homeland Defense and Civil Support." On this subject, the QRM report concluded that DoD would posture and conduct operations in order to:

> [E]nsure the integrity and security of the homeland by detecting, deterring, preventing, or if necessary defeating threats and aggression against the United States as early and as far from its borders as possible so as to minimize the effects on U.S. society and interests.[9]

There is to be sure a decidedly geographic component to the description noted earlier. Nonetheless, its core focus on "detecting, deterring, preventing, [and] defeating" hazards "so as to minimize the effects on U.S. society and interests"—in essence—captures the intent of the study team as it relates to this objective. Physical distance and boundaries do limit some challenges from materially affecting the fundamental security of the United States. However, other hazards exist in spite of them. Indeed, often these thrive because of a traditional fixation on defending against the most conventional, well-rehearsed, and well-understood hazards first.[10]

Secure Access to the Global Commons and Strategic Regions, Markets, and Resources.

The United States and its international partners rely on unimpeded access to air, sea, space, cyberspace, and the electromagnetic spectrum in order to underwrite their security and prosperity.[11] Indeed, even states and actors with which the United States has substantial disputes also benefit from the free and open use of what have been universally recognized as international common spaces and resources. All five of the aforementioned domains or environments are increasingly vulnerable to the predations of malicious nonstate actors, as well as states seeking to extend their influence and exploit obvious competitor vulnerabilities. In the process, they are increasingly limiting or constraining American freedom of action as well.

Access for access sake is obviously not enough. Routes and connections between strategic markets, marketplaces, and resources in both the physical and virtual context run through common space virtually every international actor of consequence depends on. Goods and services are distributed via physical conveyance, as well as voice or data communications. There are obstacles or chokepoints along the way that also require constant security and maintenance to ensure they facilitate vice impede the legitimate political, economic, and security business of states.

In all cases—as it applies to the commons, regions, markets, or resources—there are also profound basic security interests at play related to the concept of access. Failure of or limitations on the ability of the United States to enter and operate within key regions of the world, for example, undermine both U.S. and partner security. Challenges to access also limit or increase significantly the costs associated with the United States living up to its long-standing security commitments and curtails American influence over key regional security challenges, challengers, and outcomes. Purposeful, malevolent, or incidental interruption of access to the commons, as well as critical regions, resources, and markets are accelerating features of the post-primacy environment. As such, they remain a centerpiece of DoD strategy and risk calculations.

Meet Foreign Security Obligations.

Yet another consistent component of U.S. defense policy for the past 25 years has been an abiding American commitment to the security of treaty allies and major non-treaty international partners.[12] This near-innate responsibility for the defense of a constellation of commonly recognized and mutually supportive international partners is born as much out of an American instinct for realist self-preservation as it is selflessness. Since the end of World War II and the treaty obligations that emerged from the early Cold War period (e.g., NATO, Japan, Republic of Korea, the Philippines, Australia, and New Zealand), collective defense and security have been bedrocks of U.S. national strategy. Consequently, they underpin U.S. defense decision-making as well.[13]

By definition, traditional and emerging bi- and multi-lateral security arrangements or less formal alignments do two things for the United States. First, they guarantee meaningful and ready-made U.S. partners for confronting the most important threats to collective well-being. Second, they also promise some hope for burden-sharing—both as it applies to the former hazards to core interests, as well as to less important or peripheral challenges where overt U.S. leadership may be counter-productive and/or an other-than-U.S. lead may be preferred.

The American commitment to its foreign partners is thus a fundamental investment in U.S. security. As will be discussed in the next section, an important feature of the post-primacy environment is the increasing adherence to self-interest first among Western politicians and other U.S. allies.[14] This leaves the United States facing the prospect of being at-risk and friendless in an increasingly hostile environment where barriers to entry into effective counter-U.S. resistance are increasingly lower.

Continued adherence to traditional U.S. security commitments, and attempting through engagement to expand the community of like-minded states will serve to bolster what many recognize as an increasingly compromised U.S. position. Further, to the extent that the United States leads its partners to find and enact workable solutions to common defense and national security challenges, the more likely the United States will return to a position of decided advantage vis-à-vis its competitors. If the United States remains prone to accommodate partners and reduce collective allied anxiety, the United States will regain some lost ground internationally and will do so with the wind of strong international partnerships at its back. Failure to do so, however, is likely to result in further erosion of American position and increased strategic-level risk.[15]

Both inside and outside the United States, a great number of analysts and opinion-makers are questioning the continued strength of U.S. commitment to its commonly recognized security obligations. At the same time, the study team found through extensive interactions with key defense stakeholders that the maintenance of the U.S. position as a dominant global power is untenable without both active maintenance and expansion of meaningful security partnerships worldwide.[16]

The world has grown accustomed to U.S. leadership. Yet, there are real fears that a combination of effective counter-U.S. resistance and deliberate, unilateral U.S. hesitation and restraint have both diminished American leverage and eroded many of the key advantages essential to the United States maintaining and leading its historically strong network of alliances and partnerships.[17] According to General David Petraeus, "The paradox of the moment is that, just as the threats to the world order [the United States] created have grown ever more apparent, American resolve about its defense has become somewhat ambivalent."[18]

In the end, the study team found this objective to be at the same time potentially the United States' single greatest competitive advantage, as well as its single greatest vulnerability.[19] Going forward, senior U.S. decision-makers will need to carefully account for the strength of U.S. relationships, the reliability of individual U.S. partners, and the degree and merit of partner contributions to collective defense and security.[20]

Underwrite a Stable, Resilient, and Rules-Based International Order.

Senior U.S. decision-makers naturally feel an obligation to preserve the U.S. global position within a favorable international order while protecting the United States and its people from consequential aggression, attack, or disruption.[21] Before September 11, 2001 (9/11), this had very specific implications for DoD. Prior to 9/11, the operative international order felt comfortable to U.S. strategists, as they or their predecessors had—over the previous 55 years—largely been responsible for its construction and maintenance.[22]

Up to 9/11, that operative order was perceived to be dominated by the well-practiced, often-predictable competitive and cooperative relationships between states. In reality, while global security affairs were likely considerably more complex than perceived in the immediate post-Cold War period and through 9/11, this classically realist frame or lens was nonetheless the aperture through which U.S. policymakers and senior military leaders understood the world and its distribution of power.[23]

Since 9/11, however, U.S. perceptions of both the complexity of the contemporary order (or disorder) and its inherent hazards have grown more sophisticated, uncertain, unsettling, and confounding.[24] The next section describes the contemporary post-primacy environment in detail. While the United States still clings to significant political, economic, and military leverage, that leverage is increasingly exhibiting less reach, durability, and endurance. In short, the rules-based global order that the United States built and sustained for 7 decades is under enormous stress. The greatest source of stress lies in an inherent dynamism in the character and velocity of consequential change in strategic conditions. General Petraeus is instructive here as well. He recently observed:

> Americans should not take the current international order for granted. It did not will itself into existence. [The United States] created it. Likewise, it is not self-sustaining. [The United States has] sustained it. If [the United States] stops doing so, it will fray and, eventually, collapse.[25]

U.S. adjustment to the post-primacy era has been uneven at best. What can be perceived by foreign rivals or domestic partisan opposition as fecklessness on the part of those charged with U.S. foreign and security policy might instead simply be confusion—confusion about the proximate source and nature of consequential hazards, the risks associated with action or inaction against them, and the stability of the foundation upon which past best practice has most often ably averted military catastrophe, contagious insecurity, and uncontrolled disorder.[26]

Today, past best practice is increasingly ineffective. Revisionist or revolutionary powers such as China, Russia, Iran, and North Korea demonstrate a penchant for paralyzing, counter-U.S. gray zone competition.[27] Vulnerable states are also falling victim to more organic networked rejectionist forces and movements that effectively challenge the legitimate exercise of political authority wherever they emerge. The growth, persistent presence, and corrosive impact of these stateless environmental forces lead to noticeable spikes in terrorism, insurgency, and civil conflict, and undermine the U.S.-led order often less by purpose than by implication. In reality, the "rules" in "rules-based" are failing and the United States is struggling to keep pace.[28]

However, American military power does continue to insure or underwrite stability in critical regions of the world. And, while the favorable U.S.-dominated status quo is under significant internal and external pressure, adapted American power can help to forestall or even reverse outright failure in the most critical regions.[29] There is significantly more to effective solutions than military power. However, a broad front of hostile challenges and forces are in position to sweep the status quo aside and in the process, create conditions that are profoundly unfavorable to U.S. interests.

If the United States is to regain significant control over the most important international security outcomes, it will need to pursue a deliberate campaign that progressively re-seizes lost initiative and invests U.S. power in a remodeled but nonetheless still favorable post-primacy international order. Anticipating and adapting early to dynamic change will have a profound and positive impact on the U.S. global position. Further still, DoD will be a central player in both conceptualizing the character of and components of both the most compelling hazards to U.S. position, as well as American responses to those hazards.[30]

Build and Maintain a Favorable and Adaptive Global Security Architecture.

Securing any or all of the aforementioned objectives will require the United States to avail itself of its significant latent advantage. It does have, for example, the most extensive system of existing alliances and partnerships of any contemporary great power.[31] According to General Petraeus, "[The United States has] an extraordinary network of partners who are stakeholders in the current order and can be mobilized . . . in its defense."[32] However, as noted, those relationships are admittedly under increasing internal and external pressure. The United States would be well-served to adapt and also expand its alliances to create a more robust network of mutual support and collective security—all transcending geography, functional demand, and purposeful and contextual hazards.

Further, the United States possesses the largest and most sophisticated and integrated intelligence complex in world. With it, it can reach into the darkest most threatening corners by either or both human and high-tech collection. Leveraging the U.S. intelligence community's enormous human and technical analysis capability, the United States is also able to generate insight faster and more reliably than its competitors can, if it chooses to do so.[33]

Finally, the United States' ability to knit together into a seamless whole its substantial alliance relationships, military forward presence and power projection, intelligence **capability** and capacity, virtual reach, and its latent allure as a security partner of choice potentially leave it in an enviable position of strength. That strength, however, is only as durable as the United States' willingness to see and employ it to its advantage. To the extent that the United States and its defense enterprise are seen to lead, others will follow and contribute meaningfully to solving many of the world's most complex and threatening collective security challenges.[34]

Create, Preserve, and Extend U.S. Military Advantage and Options.

In general terms, DoD is responsible for maintaining sufficient military **capability** and **capacity** to deter threats to the nation's most important at-risk interests and successfully defend those interests when deterrence fails. This latter point will naturally involve the preservation, and when necessary commitment, of sufficient resources to defeat threats as they become more active, violent, disruptive, or destructive.

However, in reality, decisive or definitive defeat of adversaries may not always be realistic, as it may simply exceed U.S. risk and cost thresholds. This is especially true when U.S. decision-makers come face-to-face with more organic and durable rejectionist hazards. Here, defense and military leaders will face the unsatisfying requirement to contain hazards at an acceptable cost to prevent strategic exhaustion or the fatal erosion of U.S. and partner interests.

While as a rule, U.S. leaders of both political parties have consistently committed to the maintenance of U.S. military superiority over all potential state rivals, the post-primacy reality demands a wider and more flexible military force that can generate advantage and options across the broadest possible range of military demands.[35] To U.S. political leadership, maintenance of military advantage preserves maximum freedom of action. Further, it underwrites yet another bedrock principle of American defense policy—nuclear and conventional deterrence. Finally, it allows U.S. decision-makers the opportunity to dictate or hold significant sway over outcomes in international disputes in the shadow of significant U.S. military capability and the implied promise of unacceptable consequences in the event that capability is unleashed.

As will become increasingly clear in the next section, post-primacy complicates the maintenance of advantage and the preservation of workable military options. To the extent defense-relevant security challenges from both state and nonstate actors manifest as more unconventional, hybrid, or gray zone behaviors or, indeed, to the extent they emerge organically in ways that pit U.S. interests against disruptive challenges to traditional political authority, the more likely DoD will be tested to keep pace with emerging defense-relevant hazards.

If preservation of maximum freedom of action is the objective, future risk assessments at the strategic and military levels of analysis will need to account for a much broader set of threats and threat vectors. In a word, from this point forward, hazards to core interests and enduring defense objectives will be more diverse and, as a consequence, preservation and extension of U.S. military advantage will require a more nuanced and sophisticated appreciation of both the advantages and limitations of U.S. and partner military force and forces.

A Final Note on Objectives.

Noticeably absent from the lead in every enduring defense objective is reference to the usual action verbs like deter, defeat, deny, etc. The team has effectively demonstrated that these are embedded within and across all of the objectives. Securing these six objectives is critical to DoD navigating the contemporary post-primacy environment. They provide an illustrative set of strategic waypoints for effective strategy development and risk assessment. In the next section, the study team articulates the five basic characteristics of post-primacy and the defense implications of those characteristics.

ENDNOTES – SECTION IV

1. Chairman of the Joint Chiefs of Staff (CJCS), Chairman of the Joint Chiefs of Staff Manual (CJCSM) 3105.01, *Joint Risk Analysis*, Washington, DC: U.S. Department of Defense, October 14, 2016, p. C-5, available from *www.jcs.mil/Library/CJCS-Manuals/*, accessed February 2, 2017.

2. The study team examined defense strategic documents from 1993-2015. The first document examined was the *Report on the Bottom-Up Review* in 1993, followed by subsequent *Quadrennial Defense Reviews* (QDR), *National Defense Strategies* (NDS), and *National Military Strategies* (NMS) through 2015.

3. These objectives represent the majority of opinions from key risk stakeholders engaged during multiple working group sessions.

4. This insight was derived from study team engagement with senior and working-level leaders and staff officers in the U.S. Pacific Command (USPACOM) Area of Responsibility (AoR) in March 2017.

5. After three sessions of vetting objectives, the study team found that broad objectives would be more universal and translate more effectively over time.

6. These six objectives were a result of a survey of defense strategic documents that covered four Presidential administrations.

7. See General Colin Powell, *National Military Strategy of the United States*, Washington, DC: U.S. Joint Chiefs of Staff, January 1992, p. 5; Robert Gates, *National Defense Strategy*, Washington, DC: U.S. Department of Defense, June 2008, p. 6: and Chuck Hagel, *Quadrennial Defense Review 2014*, Washington, DC: U.S. Department of Defense, March 2014, p. 12, available from *archive.defense.gov/pubs/2014_Quadrennial_Defense_Review.pdf*, accessed May 3, 2017. There have been numerous instances of this objective in defense strategic documents over the last 25 years. For example, the 1992 NMS states that the United States will "Deter any aggression that could threaten the security of the United States and its allies." The 2008 NDS states, "The core responsibility of the Department of Defense [DoD] is to defend the United States from attack upon its territory at home and to secure its interests abroad." The 2014 QDR states, "Maintaining the capability to deter and defeat attacks on the United States is the Department's first priority."

8. National Intelligence Council, *Global Trends: Paradox of Progress*, Washington, DC: National Intelligence Agency, January 2017, p. 28, available from *https://www.dni.gov/files/images/globalTrends/documents/GT-Full-Report.pdf*, accessed April 3, 2017. For example, "the ability of the U.S. Armed Forces to deter acts of aggression in one or more theaters by remaining capable of decisively defeating adversaries is critical to preserving stability and is fundamental to our role as a global leader."

9. Robert Gates, *Quadrennial Roles and Missions Review Report*, Washington, DC: U.S. Department of Defense, January 2009, p. 5, available from *https://www.defense.gov/Portals/1/features/defenseReviews/QDR/QRMFinalReport_v26Jan.pdf*, accessed April 1, 2017.

10. See for example, George W. Bush, "Remarks at Naval Station Mayport in Jacksonville," February 13, 2003, available from *www.presidency.ucsb.edu/ws/index.php?pid=156*, accessed April 1, 2017. "The world changed on September the 11th, 2001. You see, we learned that oceans no longer protect us, that a threat that gathers on the other side of the Earth can strike our own cities, can kill our own people."

11. See for example, Donald Rumsfeld, *The National Defense Strategy of The United States of America*, Washington, DC: U.S. Department of Defense, 2005, p. iv, available from *archive.defense.gov/news/Mar2005/ d20050318nds1.pdf*, accessed April 1, 2017; Hagel, p. 63. For example, the 2005 NDS states, "We will promote the security, prosperity, and freedom of action of the United States and its partners by securing access to key regions, lines of communication, and the global commons." The 2014 QDR states, "Our forces will also have considerable responsibilities. They must protect allies, be globally present to deter conflict, protect the global commons, and keep war far from our shores and our citizens."

12. See for example, Donald Rumsfeld, *Quadrennial Defense Review Report*, Washington, DC: U.S. Department of Defense, September 30, 2001, p. 11; Hagel, p. 18. For example, the 2001 QDR states, "The U.S. military plays a critical role in assuring allies and friends that the Nation will honor its obligations and will be a reliable security partner." The 2014 QDR states, "Our commitment to the NATO Alliance is steadfast and resolute, and the United States will work with allies and partners to ensure NATO remains a modern and capable alliance."

13. Martin Murphy, "The Importance of Alliances for U.S. Security," in Dakota L. Wood, ed., *2017 Index of U.S. Military Strength: Assessing America's Ability to Provide for the Common Defense*, Washington, DC: The Heritage Foundation, 2016, available from *index.heritage.org/military/2017/essays/importance-alliances-us-security/*, accessed April 3, 2017.

14. See for example, Theresa May, "Speech in Philadelphia," January 26, 2017, available from *www.ibtimes.co.uk/read-theresa-mays-speech-republicans-philadelphia-full-1603339*. Prime Minister Theresa May stated, "the days of Britain and America intervening in sovereign countries in an attempt to remake the world in our own image are over." She went on to say that the UK would only intervene where there are British national interests. She goes on to say nations are accountable to their populations, and their powers are derived from the consent of the governed and they can choose to join international organizations, cooperate, or trade with whom they wish.

15. See for example, this review of *A World in Disarray: American Foreign Policy and the Crisis of the Old Order*, by Richard Haass in Michiko Kakutani, "'A World in Disarray' Is a Calm Look at a Chaotic Global Order," *The New York Times*, February 13, 2017, available from *https://www.nytimes.com/2017/02/13/books/a-world-in-disarray-richard-haass.html*, accessed April 2, 2017. Richard Haass states:

> Friends and allies who depend on the United States for their security need to know that this dependence is well placed. If America comes to be doubted, it will inevitably give rise to a very different and much less orderly world. One would see two reactions: either a world of increased 'self-help,' in which countries take matters into their own hands in ways that could work against U.S. objectives, or a world in which countries fall under the sway of more powerful local states, in the process undermining the balance of power.

16. This insight was derived from multiple sessions with the expert working group (EWG), senior working group (SWG), and other key risk stakeholders throughout the course of the study.

17. See for example, Eliot Cohen, Eric S. Edelman, and Brian Hook, "Presidential Priority: Restore American Leadership," *World Affairs*, Spring 2016, available from *www.worldaffairsjournal.org/article/presidential-priority-restore-american-leadership*, accessed April 4, 2017. The authors state, "U.S. leaders need to recognize and learn from policies that have succeeded over the past seven decades and those that have failed, but they must not lose sight of the fact that on the whole, America has served the world far better when confidently asserting power and influence than when retreating into impotence and self-doubt."

18. David H. Petraeus, "The State of the World," Testimony to House Armed Services Committee, Washington, DC, February 1, 2017, available from *docs.house.gov/meetings/AS/AS00/20170201/105509/ HHRG-115-AS00-Wstate-PetraeusD-20170201.pdf*, accessed April 23, 2017.

19. Insight gained from the EWG and SRG showed that failure to maintain alliances makes the United States vulnerable in today's environment.

20. This insight was largely derived both from EWG interaction, as well as study team engagement with senior and working-level leaders and staff officers in the USPACOM AoR. The latter occurred in both Hawaii and Japan during roundtable discussions March 6-9, 2017.

21. See Robert Gates, *Quadrennial Defense Review Report*, Washington, DC: U.S. Department of Defense, February 2010, p. iv; General Martin Dempsey, *The National Military Strategy of the United States of America 2015*, Washington, DC: U.S. Joint Chiefs of Staff, June 2015, p. 5, available from *www.jcs.mil/Portals/36/Documents/Publications/2015_National_Military_Strategy.pdf*, accessed April 4, 2017. For example, the 2010 QDR states "America's interests are inextricably linked to the integrity and resilience of the international system. Chief among these interests is security, prosperity, broad respect for universal values, and an international order that promotes cooperative action." The 2015 NMS states, "As detailed in the 2015 National Security Strategy, our enduring national interests are . . . a rules-based international order advanced by U.S. leadership that promotes peace, security, and opportunity through stronger cooperation to meet global challenges."

22. See for example, Eric A. Posner, "Sorry, America, the New World Order is Dead," *Foreign Policy*, May 6, 2014, available from *foreignpolicy.com/2014/05/06/sorry-america-the-new-world-order-is-dead/*, accessed April 3, 2017. "In the 1990s, it was possible to believe that a new international order had replaced the bipolar system of the Cold War. . . . Today, this order is breaking down, the result of the decline of U.S. power and hence America's ability to enforce its values and interests abroad."

23. Les Aspin, *Report on the Bottom-Up Review*, Washington, DC: U.S. Department of Defense, October 1993, p. iii. For example, the *Bottom-Up Review* was designed "toward the new dangers of the post-Cold War era. Chief among the new dangers is that of aggression by regional powers."

24. Rumsfeld, *The National Defense Strategy of The United States of America*, p. 2. For example, the 2005 NDS states, "Uncertainty is the defining characteristic of today's strategic environment. We can identify trends but cannot predict specific events with precision. While we work to avoid being surprised, we must posture ourselves to handle unanticipated problems—we must plan with surprise in mind."

25. Petraeus.

26. Nathan Freier, "Does Anyone Really Know What's Going On? Likely Not." Carlisle, PA: Strategic Studies Institute, U.S. Army War College, June 17, 2015, available from *ssi.armywarcollege.edu/index.cfm/articles/Does-Anyone-Really-Know-Whats-Going-On/2015/06/17*, accessed April 2, 2017.

27. Nathan Freier, proj. dir., Charles R. Burnett, William J. Cain, Jr., Christopher D. Compton, Sean M. Hankard, Robert S. Hume, Gary R. Kramlich II, J. Matthew Lissner, Tobin A. Magsig, Daniel E. Mouton, Michael S. Muztafago, James M. Schultze, John F. Troxell, and Dennis G. Wille, cont. auths., *Outplayed: Regaining Strategic Initiative in the Gray Zone*, Carlisle, PA: Strategic Studies Institute, U.S. Army War College, 2016, available from *ssi.armywarcollege.edu/pubs/display.cfm?pubID=1325*, accessed May 3, 2017.

28. See for example, "Challenges to the Rules-Based International Order," London, UK: Chatham House, 2015, available from *https://www.chathamhouse.org/london-conference-2015/background-papers/challenges-to-rules-based-international-order*, accessed April 2, 2017. This background paper describes the international system and its rules as the following: "given its antique origins, it is not surprising that this order now seems increasingly under pressure. . . . the rules need to be revised to ensure that they remain relevant, and that they need to be applied as consistently and extensively as possible."

29. See for example, Cohen, Edelman, and Hook who state:

> The American hand in international politics remains stronger than that of China or any other potential rival or collection of rivals. The United States has a modestly growing and relatively young population, unlike China, Russia, Japan, and Europe. The depth of our financial markets and research institutions remains unmatched. . . . [America is] the world's most productive [in] agriculture, natural resources, and clean air. The American military is the most experienced in the world, and although others can match individual aspects of its military capabilities, none has their full spectrum of abilities.

30. The study team recognized that many contemporary security challenges are cross-cutting whole of government issues. However, there was broad agreement among the EWG, SRG, and key stakeholders that DoD culture of planning positions it well to assist in adapting to contemporary conditions and leading others to comprehensive solutions.

31. See Gates, *Quadrennial Defense Review Report*, p. 13; Dempsey, p. 9. For example, the 2010 QDR states, "America's enduring effort to advance common interests without resort to arms is a hallmark of its stewardship of the international system. . . . Such an approach also requires working closely with our allies and partners to leverage existing alliances and create conditions to advance common interests." The 2015 NMS states, "As we look to the future, the U.S. military and its allies and partners will continue to protect and promote shared interests. We will preserve our alliances, expand partnerships, maintain a global stabilizing presence, and conduct training, exercises, security cooperation activities, and military-to-military engagement."

32. Petraeus.

33. Office of the Director of National Intelligence (ODNI), "Mission, Vision and Goals," n.d., available from *https://www.dni.gov/index.php/who-we-are/mission-vision*, accessed May 4, 2017. ODNI argues that intelligence integration is the key to the mission and vision, and includes key goals of "Integrate intelligence analysis and collection to inform decisions made from the White House to the foxhole" and "Advance cutting-edge capabilities to provide global intelligence advantage." Finally, ODNI identifies the 17 intelligence organizations under its umbrella; see ODNI, "Organization," n.d., available from *https://www.dni.gov/index.php/who-we-are/organizations*, accessed May 16, 2017.

34. See for example, Joseph Lieberman and Jon Kyl, "Why American leadership still matters," Washington, DC: American Enterprise Institute, December 3, 2015, available from *https://www.aei.org/publication/why-american-leadership-still-matters/*, accessed April 4, 2017.

35. See William S. Cohen, *Report of the Quadrennial Defense Review*, Washington, DC: U.S. Department of Defense, May 1997, p. 35; Rumsfeld, *The National Defense Strategy of The United States of America*, p. 7. For example, the 1997 QDR states, "As we move into the next century, it is imperative that the United States maintain its military superiority in the face of evolving, as well as discontinuous, threats and challenges." The 2005 NDS states, "We will work to dissuade potential adversaries from adopting threatening capabilities, methods, and ambitions, particularly by sustaining and developing our own key military advantages."

V. A POST-PRIMACY DECISION-MAKING ENVIRONMENT

> The international system is in transition from a period when things were quite clear, moving toward some new alignment for which we do not have a name or a broadly accepted guiding concept.[1]

Defense strategists and senior decision-makers should be under no illusion about the current tenuous degree to which the United States exercises meaningful control over key strategic outcomes in the international security environment. The United States and its defense enterprise are navigating uncharted waters of late. The potency, endurance, and resilience of once unassailable post-Cold War American reach, influence, and effectiveness are increasingly in doubt.

Contrary to former CIA Director John McLaughlin's statement quoted at the beginning of this chapter, the study team suggests there is a name for the current decision-making and operating environment. This report argues that the United States has recently entered, or more accurately has freshly recognized that it is in the midst of what can only be described as the early post-U.S. primacy epoch. While jarring for strategists and policymakers who are accustomed to the assumption of primacy, they will need to adapt. This new reality has far-reaching implications for American defense policy, strategy, planning, and risk calculation. From a defense strategy and planning perspective, post-primacy has five basic defining characteristics.

- Hyperconnectivity and the weaponization of information, disinformation, and disaffection.[2]
- A rapidly fracturing post-Cold War status quo.[3]
- Proliferation, diversification, and atomization of effective counter-U.S. resistance.[4]
- Resurgent but transformed great power competition.[5]
- Violent or disruptive dissolution of political cohesion and identity.[6]

In combination, these forces are fundamentally changing the strategic context within which senior defense leadership weigh various choices, assess their relative value, and gauge the risk associated with chosen courses of action.

HYPERCONNECTIVITY – SPEED KILLS

Arguably, the most transformative characteristic of the contemporary environment is the sudden onslaught of threats emerging from the dark underside of hyperconnectivity.[7] One can hardly exaggerate the degree to which hyperconnectivity enables: 1) hostile or disruptive virtual mobilization worldwide; 2) the collapse of privacy, secrecy, and operational security; 3) penetration, disruption, exploitation, and destruction of data storage and transmission, as well as the use of data and data-enabled systems; and finally, 4) the unfettered manipulation of perceptions, material outcomes, and consequential strategic decisions.

That which is loosely identified as the information sphere—indeed often wrongly characterized exclusively as the "cyber domain"—has of late become the world's most contested and congested competitive space.⁸ Indeed, while well-meaning strategists and planners work through the incredible complexity of cyber competition and conflict, the broader competitive space that revolves around information has rapidly transcended the challenges of 1s and 0s alone.⁹

On the first, second, and third points, the study makes the following basic observations. First, the proliferation of portable communications and computing devices—matched with their inevitable interconnectedness—unavoidably increases the ability of purposeful actors at and below the state level to communicate, plan, agitate, and execute profoundly disruptive acts that range from unprovoked and malicious to targeted and incredibly destructive.

Furthermore, the same connectivity also becomes a vehicle for the rapid, viral transmission of equally disruptive information, emerging more organically and triggering unanticipated, seemingly leaderless security challenges. The latter are literally unbounded, borderless, and virtually uncontrollable.¹¹ In the study team's view, the strategic significance of hyperconnectivity cannot be overstated. Currently, imagination is the only barrier to the worst possible manifestations of this increasingly complex challenge to U.S. interests and enduring defense objectives.

> *Thanks to the internet, the public can identify people with the same values and fears, exchange ideas, and build relationships faster than ever before. Our governments are simply not part of that conversation: we have 19th century institutions with 20th century mindsets, attempting to communicate with 21st century citizens. Our governments are elected, dissolved and re-elected only to pursue short-term agendas, yet the cycles that innovate and build trust with voters require long-term investment.*¹⁰

On the second point, it is clear that Americans (elite or otherwise) no longer benefit from an assumption of privacy to the extent that they are connected to the information grid. Virtually, anyone now can be found, exposed, extorted, embarrassed, robbed, harmed, or intimidated from either open or anonymous sources so long as they remain "plugged in" and active on the worldwide web.¹² With the collapse of personal privacy comes the inevitable elimination of secrecy and operational security from a national security and defense perspective as well. Wide uncontrolled access to technology that most now take for granted is rapidly undermining prior advantages of discrete, secret, or covert intentions, actions, or operations.¹³

The wide proliferation and use of cellular devices capable of high-definition recording matched to their **capability** for immediate transmission of sound, pictures, and written text is transforming both how the world gets its most up-to-date information, as well as fundamentally undermining the ability of the world's militaries and intelligence services to operate with a modicum of operational security. Furthermore, individuals, groups, and states are now able to access imagery and sensitive open source information that once was tightly controlled by governments. In the end, senior defense leaders should assume that all defense-related activity from minor tactical movements to major military operations would occur completely in the open from this point forward.¹⁴

On the third point, the secure storage, transmission, and use of data and data-enabled systems are under persistent assault. From a cyber perspective, unconnected or closed systems are frankly never completely closed.¹⁵ Open systems are literally open to all. Finally, connected but encrypted systems are in fact first "connected" and then "encrypted." They are, therefore, neither closed nor unbreachable. Consequently, state secrets, sensitive or proprietary information, and information enabled technical systems face concerted efforts to penetrate, expose, and/or manipulate them for a variety of motives. The defense-related hazards are myriad in this regard.

Recent events indicate that hyperconnectivity as it relates to the fourth point—unfettered manipulation of perceptions, material outcomes, and consequential strategic decisions—may just be the most immediately consequential. Largely free-riding on the back a metastasizing global cyber superstructure, actors are increasingly weaponizing information, disinformation, and popular disaffection in order to by-pass the traditional defenses of target states and institutions. Furthermore, the incidental or accidental weaponization of the same is increasingly creating unguided and unintended collateral effects from the strategic to tactical levels of decision and action. There are myriad examples of both impacts in the contemporary environment.[16]

As information now literally travels at light speed, it is very difficult to limit its adverse effects. Sometimes the exposure or exploitation of high-impact information is **fact-free**. Sometimes it is **fact-inconvenient**. Still other times it is **fact-perilous**. Finally, there are times that it is **fact-toxic**.

The first proliferates in ways that undermine objective truth. In short, once fact-free information is deposited in or employed through the information sphere, the real story is lost in a sea of alternative realities. George F. Kennan was prescient in this regard when he observed, "the truth is sometimes a poor competitor in the market place of ideas—complicated, unsatisfying, full of dilemmas, always vulnerable to misinterpretation and abuse."[17]

Fact-inconvenient information exposes comprising details that, by implication, undermine legitimate authority and erode the relationships between governments and the governed. Fact-perilous data gives away the keys to the castle—exposing highly classified, sensitive, or proprietary information that can be used to accelerate a real loss of tactical, operational, or strategic advantage. In addition, finally, when exposed in the absence of context, fact-toxic information poisons important political discourse and fatally weakens foundational security at an international, regional, national, or personal level. Indeed, **fact-toxic** exposures are those likeliest to trigger viral or contagious insecurity across or within borders and between or among peoples.

Thus, securing computer networks and cyber lines of communication from the predations of opportunistic opponents remains a critical component of U.S. defense calculations. However, this is essential but also insufficient in the contemporary environment. Indeed, to date, American strategists have focused to the point of distraction on defense against the purposeful interruption or destruction of the United States' information-focused connective tissue, as well as intrusion into and damage to sensitive information repositories. However, consequently, they have been less focused on the purposeful exploitation of the same architecture for the strategic manipulation of perceptions and its attendant influence on political and security outcomes.[18]

This idea of the grid as a vulnerability, a vector, and a weapon is an important future risk consideration for the Department of Defense (DoD). Further, the ongoing revolution in connectivity will continue to transform how DoD perceives and responds to hazards and calculates the risk factors related to all three considerations.

The study team suggests there is a single core defense implication of hyperconnectivity—"speed kills." With hyperconnectivity comes a quantum increase in the velocity of change in strategic circumstances. It raises the specter of sudden, violent, or disruptive political contagions; rapid, unintended military escalation; as well as war prosecuted by alternative—even overtly non-violent—means at increasingly faster processing speeds. Furthermore, it enables virtual mobilization and distributed collective action under no centralized authority or control and at speeds that will outpace 20th-century bureaucracies at every turn.

FRACTURING POST-COLD WAR STATUS QUO—FOUR FORCES, "OLD WORLD" ARTIFACTS, AND THE RISE OF SELF-INTEREST

As was described earlier in this report, the stability, surety, and resilience of the U.S.-led post-Cold War status quo is under severe distress and faces potential collapse. This was the first operative assumption articulated in last year's U.S. Army War College (USAWC) report, *Outplayed: Regaining Strategic Initiative in the Gray Zone*.[19] According to the authors of that report, "The U.S. led status quo will remain under persistent assault from a diverse array of actors, forces, and conditions."[20]

Consistent with *Outplayed*, this year's study team determined that the unrelenting pressure on the U.S.-led status quo was the result of a collision and interaction among and between four major competitive forces: status quo, revisionist, rejectionist, and revolutionary. Three of the four—status quo, revisionist, and rejectionist forces—were identified last year in *Outplayed*.[21] This year's study group added the fourth—revolutionary.[22]

This study identified four competing post-primacy forces:
- ***Status Quo***: *Values the distribution of power and authority and intends to maintain it.*
- ***Revisionist***: *Benefits from the current order but seeks a meaningful redistribution of power and authority in their favor.*
- ***Revolutionary***: *Seeks a wholly different order within which they can exercise control over their immediate sphere of influence without interference.*
- ***Rejectionist***: *Rejects current order, actively seeks to undermine it and any that might try to maintain or exercise control of it.*

As a review, status quo forces benefit from and act as the self-appointed guardians of the U.S.-led post-Cold War international order and its components.[23] *Outplayed* described status quo forces as international actors that "value the current order and actively work to secure it to their advantage."[24] The order and its constituent parts, first emerged from World War II, were transformed to a unipolar system with the collapse of the Soviet Union, and have by-and-large been dominated by the United States and its major Western and Asian allies since. Status quo forces collectively are comfortable with their dominant role in dictating the terms of international security outcomes and resist the emergence of rival centers of power and authority.[25]

Revisionist forces benefit from the same basic international order but believe they have a rightful place at the table in the negotiation and determination of the precise terms of that order going forward. In short, they seek a new distribution of power and authority commensurate with their emergence as legitimate rivals to U.S. dominance. In the current environment, Russia and China are the most obvious examples of revisionist powers. Both are engaged in a deliberate program to demonstrate the limits of U.S. authority, will, reach, influence, and impact.[26] According to *Outplayed*, "[R]evisionists advocate and agitate for a more favorable redistribution of influence and authority . . . and demonstrate a willingness to act with purpose and volition to achieve it."[27]

Revolutionary forces are neither the products of, nor are they satisfied with, the contemporary order. They lie outside for a variety of political, cultural, and historical reasons. At a minimum, they intend to destroy the reach of the U.S.-led order into what they perceive to be their legitimate sphere of influence. They are also resolved to replace that order locally with a new rule set dictated by them. Iran and North Korea may be seen as the best current examples of revolutionary forces in action.

Rejectionist forces offer very little in the way of legitimate political alternatives. Rejectionism is just as it sounds—the outright violent or disruptive rejection of legitimate political authority regardless of who happens to exercise it. Rejectionists seek to destroy formal sources of political power, especially those perceived to represent existential threats to their freedom of action.

Of all the forces at play, the rejectionists are largely represented by various nonstate, sub-state, and transnational entities and movements that pray on the current vulnerability or rejection of contemporary political convention and tradition.[28] They free-ride on hyperconnectivity to mobilize adherents around radical, criminal, or fundamentally unconventional sources of inspiration, and their reach is increasingly limited only by the number of disaffected willing to listen to and act on their various messages. Again, according to *Outplayed*:

> [Rejectionists] are largely destroyers not builders. . . . They self-identify as profoundly aggrieved, denied, or disenfranchised. Rejectionists are keen to confront what they perceive to be the unfair and illegitimate exercise of status quo political authority and they are loathe to accept a new, revisionist-led status quo that might also profit at their expense.[29]

There are profound defense implications inherent in this important post-primacy characteristic. In sum, DoD tends to target known revisionist, rejectionist, and revolutionary actors and forces before coming to terms with what appears to be a more inexorable and fundamental change in the international security environment. Where U.S. strategists tend to see the need to bandage individual wounds, others see multiple organ failure and an associated requirement for a more radical and comprehensive treatment plan. Paraphrasing one senior review group (SRG) member, it is difficult to administer an essential 25-year course of antibiotics when consequential defense decisions are made four or eight years at a time.[30] The collision of the four competitive forces is changing the origin and character of defense-relevant hazards and, thus, the conceptual and material defense responses to them.

The study team concluded that the status quo that virtually all U.S. strategy rests on is, in fact, an artifact of a prior era. It lingers precisely because it comports well with the U.S. self-image of a matchless global leader. In reality, it is an increasingly flawed foundation for forward-looking defense strategy and risk assessment under post-primacy conditions.

Current defense bias and convention are products of this flawed foundation and draw inspiration from an era where U.S. reach and influence were far less tenuous than they are today. The new reality sees senior American defense and military leaders having to work harder to secure at-risk objectives than at any time in recent memory.

A final implication rests in the fundamental uncertainty associated with post-primacy. Many states and peoples are operating under a renewed commitment to self-interest over any notions of collective common good. This more Hobbesian worldview makes alliance building and maintenance challenging. Further, to the extent this trend is operative in the United States relative to its relationships with the rest of the world, it will naturally appear more threatening to some and less attractive as a partner to others.[32]

> The future security environment will be defined by twin overarching challenges. A range of competitors will confront the United States and its global partners and interests. Contested norms will feature adversaries that credibly challenge the rules and agreements that define the international order. Persistent disorder will involve certain adversaries exploiting the inability of societies to provide functioning, stable, and legitimate governance. Confrontations involving contested norms and persistent disorder are likely to be violent, but also include a degree of competition with a military dimension short of traditional armed conflict.[31]

Indeed, the study team concluded that increasing trends toward what the current administration calls "economic nationalism" and its election on the back of a more inward looking brand of populism are themselves sources of pressure on the U.S.-led status quo.[33] If so, then there is a delicate recalibration of enduring defense objectives that would inevitably have to take place in order to effectively gauge contemporary **strategic** and **military risk**.

PROLIFERATING COUNTER-U.S. RESISTANCE — HOME FIELD ADVANTAGE FOR THEM, NO FIELD ADVANTAGE FOR US

It may be increasingly apparent to the report's consumers that the post-primacy case presented thus far is additive and compounding. As the world becomes increasingly connected, it draws the like-minded together while also exposing wide ideological and material fissures between various competitive actors and forces. In the end, three of the four dominant competitive forces at work in the international system are, in effect, militating against the effective maintenance of a U.S. position of influence.

> Today's global security environment is the most unpredictable I have seen in 40 years of service . . . global disorder has significantly increased while some of our comparative advantages [have] begun to erode. We now face multiple, simultaneous security challenges from traditional state actors and transregional networks of sub-state groups — all taking advantage of rapid technological change.[34]

All three have profound implications for defense strategy and risk assessment. And, further, as the United States itself experiences what can only be described as a period of introspection about its role in the world, its vulnerabilities to the predacious behaviors of adaptive adversaries acting with intent, as well as the arbitrary hazards of an extremely complex security environment grow more profound and variegated.

Essentially, senior defense and military leaders, strategists, and planners should recognize that the United States is in an era of persistent competition and conflict with capable, enervating forces operating at the system, state, transnational, and sub-national levels. These collectively challenge American influence and authority by design, happenstance, accident, and opportunity.

For example, the United States is in direct competition with revisionist great powers like China and Russia who have discovered complicated military and non-military work-arounds to limit U.S. freedom of action, drive up U.S. risk perceptions, and erode American reach. At the same time, mid-level revolutionary powers like Iran and North Korea present the United States with similar complex "gray zone" challenges.[35] These manifest largely on a regional basis as both direct sophisticated military threats, as well as more destabilizing, surreptitious manipulation of fragile political balances within and between vulnerable states and peoples.[36]

As each of these play out and on still other levels, the United States is buffeted by hostile, inhospitable, or uncertain networks, movements, and/or environmental disturbances manifesting as organized and purposeful resistance (e.g., Islamic State of Iraq and Syria [ISIS] and al-Qaeda) on the one hand and leaderless instability (e.g., Arab Spring) on the other. The former threatens core U.S. interests and enduring defense objectives directly, the latter by implication. All are part of a generalized disintegration of traditional authority structures (discussed shortly), fueled, and/or accelerated by hyperconnectivity and the obvious decay and potential failure of the post-Cold War status quo. While the most prominent of these forces currently emanate from the greater Middle East, it would be unwise not to recognize that they will mutate, metastasize, and manifest differently over time. Thus, it is imperative for the creation of an objective-based vice threat-based risk model.

Finally, it is impossible not to recognize the profound atomization of resistance as well. The United States and its population are increasingly exposed to substantial harm and an erosion of security from individuals and small groups of motivated actors, leveraging the confluence of hyperconnectivity, fear, and increased vulnerability to sow disorder and uncertainty. This intensely disorienting and dislocating form of resistance to authority arrives via physical, virtual, and psychological violence and can create effects that appear substantially out of proportion to the origin and physical size or scale of the proximate hazard or threat.

> Both [Russia and China], as well as other strategic cultures, envision a more complex continuum of cooperation, competition, collaboration, and conflict. Moreover, many other nations do not organize their government institutions with the same black-and-white military and non-military distinctions as the U.S. maintains.[37]

Without a sophisticated and nuanced approach to strategy and risk assessment, the proliferation, diversification, and atomization of counter-U.S. resistance will overwhelm DoD's convention and bias. It will expose substantial U.S. military **capability** to serial "capacity tests" that are bound to either fail or result in substantial losses or costs. The sources, vectors, and types of consequential hazards to enduring defense objectives equate to a persistent home field advantage for U.S. adversaries and "no field advantage"—or ceaseless disadvantage—for the U.S. defense enterprise under virtually all foreseeable contingency circumstances. High-end U.S. military advantage will continue to erode as the United States struggles to translate global reach into local superiority. At the same time, the U.S. homeland, individual American citizens, and U.S. public opinion and perceptions will increasingly become battlefields.

All of this speaks to a need for relentless adaptation to changes in the nature and character of competition and conflict. The degree to which contemporary defense-relevant hazards persistently defy expectations and conventions indicates that there is insufficient dynamism in the contemporary defense outlook.

RESURGENT GREAT POWER COMPETITION—GO GRAY OR GO HOME

As discussed earlier, the United States faces new and meaningful opposition from at least two great powers who are bent on revising the contemporary status quo. China and Russia are engaged in purposeful campaign-like activities that are focused on the material reduction of American influence as the principal arbiter of consequential international outcomes.[38] They seek to reorder their position in the existing status quo in ways that—at a minimum—create more favorable circumstances for pursuit of their core objectives. However, a more maximalist perspective sees them pursuing advantage at the direct expense of the United States and its principal Western and Asian allies.[39]

Each possesses substantial conventional and nuclear military capability. Further, each is aggressively pursuing interests in direct contravention of international norms and in ways that are threatening to U.S. and allied interests. Finally, both have adopted complex "gray zone" approaches that to date have vexed U.S. national security and defense leadership.

According to *Outplayed*, these "gray zone" approaches exhibit three common characteristics: hybridity, menace to defense/military convention, and risk confusion.[40] The latter—"risk confusion"—generates paralysis among U.S. defense and national security decision-makers in the face of this kind of opposition. *Outplayed* describes "risk confusion" this way: "threats emerging from the gray zone have a decidedly disruptive effect on **strategic risk** calculations. Often, the risk associated with action and inaction appears to be equally high and unpalatable."[41]

Thus, while the United States faces a clear resurgent great power challenge, the nature and character of that challenge is not a mirror image of past—especially Cold War—competition. Contemporary great power antagonism instead occurs principally in the "gray zone" where U.S. adversaries' substantial military capabilities are sidelined, over the horizon, or only marginally employed, but deter more activist U.S. responses nonetheless. Meanwhile, the principal competition occurs in murkier, less obvious forms of state-based aggression, where "rival states marshal various instruments of influence and intimidation to achieve warlike ends through means and methods falling far short of unambiguous or open provocation and conflict."[42]

One expert engaged during the research aptly characterized these gray zone approaches as effectively deterring the United States with one set of methods and capabilities while operating against and securing objectives at the expense of the United States using wholly different methods and capabilities.[43] While this is true, the persistent threat of escalation and the ability of both the Chinese and Russians to generate—at a minimum—niche local advantage vis-à-vis U.S. and allied forces can create paralyzing risk dilemmas for U.S. decision-makers when confronted with their activist gray zone approaches. As one expert working group (EWG) member observed with respect to the Russians in particular, their approach is to "escalate to de-escalate."[44] The implied consequence is "risk confusion," whereby future objectives-based risk assessment must account for this form of new-age great power rivalry where military capabilities and force are important, but insufficient components of effective competition.

Accordingly, the study team concluded that the United States must "go gray or go home" in defense strategy development and risk calculation. Gray zone challenges manifest as more than military threats. Indeed, the military component of gray zone threats is often the subtle menace of unacceptable cost delivered from "sanctuary" over the horizon. Nonetheless, there are very real military and security components of effective counter-gray zone activities or campaigns. Moreover, these are likely best understood and designed within the context of defense and military strategy.

The gray zone challenge is widely recognized in defense and military circles.[45] Furthermore, it has to date proven widely effective against traditional U.S. approaches to military competition. In short, U.S./partner responses to gray zone threats are to date woefully inadequate.

A more sophisticated understanding of the creeping damage associated with inaction in the face of gray zone competition will enable more coherent U.S. and partner responses to it. While the ultimate answer lies across instruments of national power and not with U.S. and allied militaries alone, it is likely that defense and military strategy and concepts will need to lead others to join into a more unified approach.

DISSOLUTION OF POLITICAL COHESION AND IDENTITY—PERSISTENT CONFLICT 2.0 WHILE "WRESTLING ON QUICKSAND"

As the United States and its foreign partners adapted to a war with Islamic extremists in the aftermath of 9/11, and as insurgencies raged in Iraq and Afghanistan, the term "persistent conflict" or "an era of persistent conflict" grew popular in Pentagon lexicon.[46] At the time, that phrase had a very particular meaning. It implied that the United States had entered an era where peace as it was previously conceived of—the complete absence of violent conflict—would no longer be the norm.

The logic held that instead the United States faced a protracted war against irregular forces and actors who were inspired by perversion of a legitimate religious ideology to pursue destructive political ends. Employing the language of this and the previous "gray zone" report, they were rejectionists, seeking to destroy a status quo order that they perceived as illegitimate and oppressive.

The fracturing of the post-Cold War global system is accompanied by the internal fraying in the political, social, and economic fabric of practically all states.[47]

The United States and its partners had indeed entered an era of persistent conflict. A survey of U.S. military commitments around the world still largely mirrors the perceived sources of extremist violence that came home to visit horror on the United States 16 years ago. However, the fight to contain or manage the Islamic extremist threat is no longer the only branch of persistent conflict confronting activist great powers like the United States today.

First and following the logic outlined thus far, all states and traditional political authority structures are under increasing pressure from endogenous and exogenous forces. The sources of that pressure are undermining the effective or legitimate exercise of political power worldwide. Sources of pressure include aspects of all of the aforementioned post-primacy characteristics including hyperconnectivity, the weaponization of information and disinformation, rapid deterioration of the post-Cold War status quo, the proliferation and diversification of meaningful resistance, the emergence of gray zone methods, and the rise of distributed sources of allegiance and identity. Paraphrasing one SRG member, some are fighting globalization and globalization is also actively fighting back.[48] Combined, all of these forces are rending at the fabric of security and stable governance that all states aspire to and rely on for survival.

The United States is not immune in this regard. Moreover, while weak states may be particularly vulnerable to acute disruption as a result of the dissolution of political cohesion, the United States and its partners are vulnerable to a greater or lesser extent as well. So too are the United States' principal rivals.

The defense implications of this trend are clear. First, employing language originally introduced in *Outplayed*, all states great and small are increasingly "wrestling on quicksand."[49] In sum, the nexus of hyperconnectivity, distributed sources of identity and allegiance, profound discontent, and political factionalism are merging with access to the means of meaningful resistance, harm, and disruption to dangerous effect. Therefore, while the United States and China compete for Pacific primacy, for example, they do so on a less stable political foundation than in the past. Moreover, this reality holds for virtually all states regardless of their inherent stability, political orientation, external alignment, or foreign activism.

Second, senior U.S. defense and military leaders should recognize that they have entered a period of "Persistent Conflict 2.0." The new post-primacy era of constant competition and conflict will witness meaningful struggles for political power and primacy occurring simultaneously at multiple levels between, within, and across states. Consequential conflict will no longer be confined to wars between states or between large rival constituencies within states. Instead, it will transcend boundaries, emerge from widely diverse motivations; persist on the back of inconvenient, incorrect, toxic, or perilous information; and finally, it will be waged with an unbounded and diverse tool set that will persistently defy conventional security wisdom. Warning of its onset will often be ambiguous or unrecognizable until hostilities are well-underway as well.

Finally, Persistent Conflict 2.0 will see states "at war" or in dispute with each other while motivated constituencies within the same states contest both the political authority of rival groups and the central government at the same time. Furthermore, like-minded, geographically distributed resistance will emerge via virtual mobilization to further contest traditional authority by employing and liberally mixing violence, disruption, and destruction under no central or formal command and control.

As the Pentagon contemplates future strategy and risk, it will need to come to terms with a generalized erosion or dissolution of traditional authority structures. To date, U.S. strategists have been fixated on this trend in the greater Middle East. However, the same forces at work there are similarly eroding the reach and authority of governments worldwide.

In light of this report's articulation of enduring defense objectives and the characteristics of the post-primacy decision-making environment, the forthcoming section outlines a new risk concept, organized around four governing principles: **diver-**

sity, **dynamism, persistent dialogue**, and **adaptation**. This new risk perspective starts with the identification of a principal risk portfolio against which DoD evaluates its **capability, capacity,** and **agility** to secure at-risk defense objectives.

ENDNOTES – SECTION V

1. John E. McLaughlin, "The State of the World: National Security Threats and Challenges," Statement before the Committee on Armed Services, Washington, DC: U.S. House of Representatives, February 1, 2017, available from *docs.house.gov/meetings/AS/AS00/20170201/105509/HHRG-115-AS00-Wstate-McLaughlinJ-20170201.pdf*, accessed April 24, 2017.

2. David W. Barno, "Silicon, Iron, And Shadow - Three Wars that will define America's future," *Foreign Policy*, March 19, 2013, available from *https://www.foreignpolicy.com/2013/03/19/silicon-iron-and-shadow*, accessed January 10, 2017.

3. Richard Haass, *A World in Disarray: American Foreign Policy and the Crisis of the Old World Order*, New York: Penguin Press, 2017.

4. Nathan Freier, proj. dir., Charles R. Burnett, William J. Cain, Jr., Christopher D. Compton, Sean M. Hankard, Robert S. Hume, Gary R. Kramlich II, J. Matthew Lissner, Tobin A. Magsig, Daniel E. Mouton, Michael S. Muztafago, James M. Schultze, John F. Troxell, and Dennis G. Wille, cont. auths., *Outplayed: Regaining Strategic Initiative in the Gray Zone*, Carlisle, PA: Strategic Studies Institute, U.S. Army War College, 2016, p. 19, available from *ssi.armywarcollege.edu/pubs/display.cfm?pubID=1325*, accessed May 3, 2017.

5. Mathew J. Burrows, "Global Risks 2035: The Search for a New Normal," *Atlantic Council Strategy Papers*, Washington, DC: Atlantic Council, September 2016, p. v.

6. *Ibid.*, p. 6.

7. Anabel Quan-Haase and Barry Wellman, "Networks of Distance and Media: A Case Study of a High-Tech Firm," paper presented at the "Trust and Communities Conference," Bielefeld, Germany, July 2003.

8. Louis Columbus, "Roundup Of Internet of Things Forecasts And Market Estimates, 2016," *Forbes*, November 27, 2016, available from *www.forbes.com/sites/louiscolumbus/2016/11/27/roundup-of-internet-of-things-forecasts-and-market-estimates-2016/#bcaa1034ba55*, accessed January 10, 2017.

9. Colonel (COL) Joseph Felter, Ret., "It's Not Just The Technology: Beyond Offset Strategies," *Strategika*, Iss. 39, March 15, 2017, available from *www.hoover.org/research/its-not-just-technology-beyond-offset-strategies*, accessed March 18, 2017.

10. Jorge Soto, "The weakening of representative democracy," in Global Agenda Councils, *Outlook on the Global Agenda 2015*, Geneva, Switzerland: World Economic Forum, 2014.

11. "The Arab Spring: A Year of Revolution," *All Things Considered*, National Public Radio (NPR), December 17, 2011, transcript available from *www.npr.org/2011/12/17/143897126/the-arab-spring-a-year-of-revolution*, accessed March 21, 2017.

12. Nicole Perlroth, "Hackers Used New Weapons to Disrupt Major Websites Across U.S.," *The New York Times*, October 21, 2016, available from *https://www.nytimes.com/2016/10/22/business/internet-problems-attack.html*, accessed December 18, 2016.

13. Columbus.

14. Patrick Tucker, "ISIS Has a Drone Strategy Too," *The Atlantic*, October 18, 2016, available from *www.theatlantic.com/technology/archive/2016/10/anti-drone/504479/*, accessed January 8, 2017.

15. Berndt Brehmer, "The Dynamic OODA Loop: Amalgamating Boyd's OODA Loop and the Cybernetic Approach to Command and Control," paper presented at 10th International Command and Control Symposium: The Future of C2, p. 2, available from *www.dodccrp.org/events/10th_ICCRTS/CD/papers/365.pdf*.

16. For example, "The Arab Spring: A Year Of Revolution," December 17, 2011.

17. George F. Kennan, *American Diplomacy*, Chicago: University of Chicago Press, 1984, p. 62.

18. Senator Rob Portman, "Senate Passes Major Portman-Murphy Counter-Propaganda Bill as Part of NDAA," December 8, 2016, available from *www.portman.senate.gov/public/index.cfm?p=press-releases&id=3765A225-B773-4F57-B21A-A265F4B5692C*.

19. Freier *et al.*, *Outplayed*, p. 12.

20. *Ibid.*, p. 19.

21. *Ibid.*

22. The addition of the "revolutionary" category grew from debates during last year's gray zone study. At that time, the study team perceived Iran to present a different set of competitive challenges than was described in either the "revisionist" or the "rejectionist" descriptions.

23. Freier *et al.*, *Outplayed*, p. 19.

24. *Ibid.*

25. *Ibid.*

26. See for example, Michael Mazarr, *Mastering the Gray Zone: Understanding a Changing Era of Conflict*, Carlisle, PA: Strategic Studies Institute, U.S. Army War College, 2015, pp. 11, 25-26, available from *ssi.armywarcollege.edu/pubs/display.cfm?pubID=1303*, accessed April 4, 2017.

27. Freier *et al.*, *Outplayed*, p. 19.

28. *Ibid.*, p. 20.

29. *Ibid.*

30. This insight emerged from one senior review group (SRG) participant at National Defense University in Washington, DC on March 30, 2017.

31. U.S. Joint Chiefs of Staff (JCS), *The Joint Operating Environment (JOE) 2035: The Joint Force in a Contested and Disordered World*, Washington, DC: U.S. Joint Chiefs of Staff, July 14, 2016.

32. This insight emerged from one SRG discussion at National Defense University in Washington, DC on March 30, 2017.

33. See for example, Daniel W. Drezner, "Who benefits from Bannon's economic nationalism?" *The Washington Post*, February 7, 2017, available from *https://www.washingtonpost.com/posteverything/wp/2017/02/07/who-benefits-from-bannons-economic-nationalism/?utm_term=.b887f7e98e1c*, accessed April 4, 2017.

34. General Martin Dempsey, *The National Military Strategy of the United States of America 2015*, Washington, DC: U.S. Joint Chiefs of Staff, June 2015, p. i, available from *www.jcs.mil/Portals/36/Documents/Publications/2015_National_Military_Strategy.pdf*, accessed April 4, 2017.

35. In the course of this study, the team added the term "revolutionary" to the existing terms status quo, revisionist, and rejectionist that were used in the earlier U.S. Army War College (USAWC) gray zone report, *Outplayed: Regaining Strategic Initiative in the Gray Zone*.

36. See for example, William J. Burns, Michèle A. Flournoy, and Nancy E. Lindborg, "U.S. Leadership and the Challenge of State Fragility," Washington, DC: Carnegie Endowment for International Peace, September 2016, p. 7, available from *carnegieendowment.org/files/US-Leadership-and-the-Challenge-of-State-Fragility.pdf*, accessed January 23, 2017.

37. Dr. Frank G. Hoffman, "The Contemporary Spectrum of Conflict: Protracted, Gray Zone, Ambiguous, and Hybrid Modes of War," in Dakota L. Wood, ed., *2016 Index of U.S. Military Strength: Assessing America's Ability to Provide for the Common Defense*, Washington, DC: The Heritage Foundation, 2015, available from *index.heritage.org/military/2016/essays/contemporary-spectrum-of-conflict/*, accessed April 3, 2017.

38. See for example, Derek Chollet, Eric Edelman, Michèle Flournoy, Stephen J. Hadley, Martin Indyk, Bruce Jones, Robert Kagan, Kristen Silverberg, Jake Sullivan, and Thomas Wright, *Building 'Situations of Strength': A National Security Strategy for the United States*, Washington, DC: The Brookings Institute, February 2017, pp. 18-23, available from *https://www.brookings.edu/research/building-situations-of-strength/*, accessed April 4, 2017.

39. See for example, Dakota L. Wood, ed., *2017 Index of U.S. Military Strength: Assessing America's Ability to Provide for the Common Defense*, Washington, DC: The Heritage Foundation, 2016, available from *index.heritage.org/military/2017/*, accessed May 13, 2017. The 2017 Index assesses the Russian and Chinese threat to U.S. vital interests to be "high." It further describes both Russia and China as purposeful and "aggressive" actors who directly challenge U.S. and allied nation interests in their respective regions, actively seek to diminish U.S. regional and global influence, and demonstrate "formidable" and "gathering" capability (using multiple ways—diplomatic, information, military, and economic) to subvert U.S. international efforts.

40. Freier *et al.*, *Outplayed*, p. 4.

41. *Ibid.*

42. *Ibid.*

43. Insight derived from a roundtable engagement with representatives from the RAND Corporation at Carlisle Barracks, PA, February 16, 2017.

44. Insight derived from a senior service strategist during the course of the third expert working group (EWG) discussion at National Defense University in Washington, DC, on January 25, 2017.

45. The Chairman of Joint Chiefs of Staff (CJCS), General Joseph Dunford, describes an environment of adversarial competition with a military dimension. See "Dunford: Challenges Require More Than 'Buying New Hardware'," Association of the United States Army, October 5, 2016, available from *https://www.ausa.org/news/dunford-challenges-require-more-%E2%80%98buying-new-hardware%E2%80%99*, accessed May 13, 2017.

46. See for example, General (GEN) George W. Casey, "The Army's Manpower and Equipment Needs in Iraq and Afghanistan," address given to the National Press Club Luncheon, Washington, DC, August 14, 2007, available from *https://www.press.org/sites/default/files/070814gcasey.pdf*, accessed April 4, 2017; Donald H. Rumsfeld, *The National Defense Strategy of The United States of America*, Washington, DC: U.S. Department

of Defense, March 2005, pp. 2-4, available from *edocs.nps.edu/dodpubs/topic/defensestrategy/2005/nms2005.pdf*, accessed April 4, 2017. While GEN Casey is often credited with coining the term "era of persistent conflict" in 2007, the concepts behind the "persistent conflict" were foundational in the development of the 2005 *National Defense Strategy* (NDS); for more complete descriptions of irregular and catastrophic challenges, see pages 2-4.

47. Burrows, p. ii.

48. This insight emerged from SRG consultations at the National Defense University in Washington, DC on March 30, 2017.

49. Freier *et al.*, *Outplayed*, p. 16.

ASSESSING AND COMMUNICATING RISK

VI. A POST-PRIMACY RISK CONCEPT: DIVERSITY, DYNAMISM, PERSISTENT DIALOGUE, AND ADAPTATION

In the emerging global landscape, rife with surprise and discontinuity, the states and organizations most able to exploit . . . opportunities will be those that are resilient, enabling them to adapt to changing conditions, persevere in the face of unexpected adversity, and take actions to recover quickly. They will invest in infrastructure, knowledge, and relationships that allow them to manage shock.[1]

CRITICAL UNANSWERED QUESTIONS

This report has been clear from the outset. It is not a direct critique of existing risk judgments. Rather, it offers alternative perspectives on **strategic** and **military risk** considerations likeliest to impact the success of the Department of Defense (DoD) in securing enduring defense objectives. Further, the U.S. Army War College (USAWC) study team deliberately avoided offering an alternative formal risk assessment framework, construct, or checklist. Frankly, the team judged this to be both unhelpful in the current environment, as well as exceeding the team's time and resource constraints.

Instead, the study offers senior DoD leadership an alternative post-primacy risk concept. This concept is intended to provide senior defense and military leadership with a fresh start point from which to begin a more fulsome post-primacy risk discourse. In effect, the report suggests that risk identification and assessment are all part of a persistent, well-structured, strategy-focused discussion at the highest levels of DoD decision-making.

The new concept accounts for risk on two important axes. The first is the vertical axis or the continuum linking **strategic** and **military risk**. The former—**strategic risk**—renders top-down judgments on the legitimacy or accuracy of DoD's overall focus or azimuth, embodied in what this study calls DoD's principal risk portfolio. The latter—**military risk**—is the more practiced bottom-up assessment of DoD's **capability** and **capacity** to succeed at an acceptable price point in performing the aggregate or discrete demands captured in the same portfolio. The portfolio was introduced previously in Section III and is described in great detail next.

This study identified four governing principles for post-primacy risk assessment—Diversity, Dynamism, Persistent Dialogue, and Adaptation:

- *Diversity in the hazards and responses considered;*
- *Acknowledgment of the inherent dynamism of DoD's contemporary decision-making environment;*
- *Persistent high-level dialogue on risk and risk management; and finally,*
- *A commitment to risk-based defense adaptation as a by-product of that persistent dialogue.*

The second horizontal access is also a continuum. It also considers DoD risks at the same two levels of analysis (**strategic** and **military**). However, it does so over time; from now through some agreed-upon future aim point. This axis runs horizontally from **operational risk** to **future challenges risk**. In defense parlance, **operational risk** is an informed judgment on DoD's ability to "fight (or respond effectively) tonight" or more accurately in the near-term (essentially, 0 to 5 years), whereas **future challenges risk** renders similar judgments about the likelihood of failure or excessive cost, but against a set of postulated future demands (in the context of this study, out to 10 years).[2]

For its part, the study found no reason to alter the labels DoD uses for the terminal ends of either axis. It does offer, however, a different perspective on the strategic and military levels of analysis, as well as the conceptual dead space currently lying along both axes. There are, after all, critical unanswered questions associated with this dead space in DoD's current risk assessment conventions.

When and how, for example, does **operational risk** transition into **future challenges risk**? Further, if **strategic risk** is about the basic direction of DoD, are there better indicators of prospective failure or excessive cost (that can be detected earlier) other than the sudden emergence of disastrous strategic surprise or shock? Likewise, if traditional military threats posed by China, Russia, Iran, or North Korea drive contemporary risk assessment, how does DoD meaningfully explore the risk associated with very real demands likely to emerge from other sources? Finally, if post-primacy hazards to **enduring defense objectives** emerge at the strategic and military levels of analysis in ways and at speeds that outplay and outpace DoD's **capability, capacity,** and **agility,** how does DoD retool risk assessment to account for its obvious challenges in keeping up?

In the end, the study team concluded that the new concept offered herein provides a number of salient considerations that are applicable to making effective risk judgments along either the strategic/military or operational/future challenges axes. Further, the study team would suggest that the report helps clarify the dead space and the unanswered questions outlined in this section.

TWO CERTAINTIES

The new post-primacy risk concept offered here is specifically intended to address what the study team believes are yawning gaps in contemporary risk identification and assessment. It proceeds from two basic certainties the team found operative at every level or point of analysis.

The first certainty is the study's unshakeable recognition that risk does not exist in a vacuum. Moreover, it certainly does not exist in a sterile, highly-controlled and predictable environment. On the first point, what commonly passes now for risk in many public and private sector planning environments is in fact simply some raw expression of hazards or unfavorable developments that may emerge from the environment. Hazards in the absence of meaningful institutional objectives, possible response demands or courses of action, and organizational priorities are not by themselves an indication of risk.

The latter point is simple acknowledgement of the diverse and dynamic hazard and demand environment DoD confronts every day. Every action—red, black, gray, green, or blue—changes conditions and alters the decision-making landscape for DoD senior leadership. Consequently, risk and risk assessment need to be agile concepts that account for and keep pace with persistent change in strategic conditions.

The second certainty holds that risk identification and assessment should be the products of uncomplicated, but at the same time not unsophisticated, frames of reference. In short, any new risk concept needs to be both widely consumable across a broad community of influential stakeholders in and out of the Pentagon, while still adequately elastic and adaptable enough to account for a strategic environment that is far more complex and dynamic than that faced by DoD in either the immediate post-Cold War or post-9/11 periods.

FOUR GOVERNING PRINCIPLES OF POST-PRIMACY RISK ASSESSMENT

The study recommends a simple parsimonious approach to both **strategic** and **military risk,** employing four basic governing principles (see Figure VI-1). The first is **diversity** in the hazards and associated defense demands considered in risk assessment by senior leaders. The second is recognition of the inherent **dynamism** in the character, **importance,** and **urgency** of DoD's current and projected **capability, capacity,** and organizational **agility** to respond to a fluid decision-making environment. The third concept—**persistent dialogue**—specifically encourages senior defense leadership to engage in a deliberate, sophisticated, and structured discussion to account for and adapt to the aforementioned diverse and dynamic aspects of the decision-making environment. A fourth and final concept is a commitment to constant risk-based **adaptation**. This includes routine risk choices like avoidance, acceptance, transfer, and mitigation. However, in light of the velocity of change in the post-primacy environment, current conceptions of these ideas may be too conservative.[3] In short, the era of marginal or incremental adjustment may be void under many post-primacy circumstances.

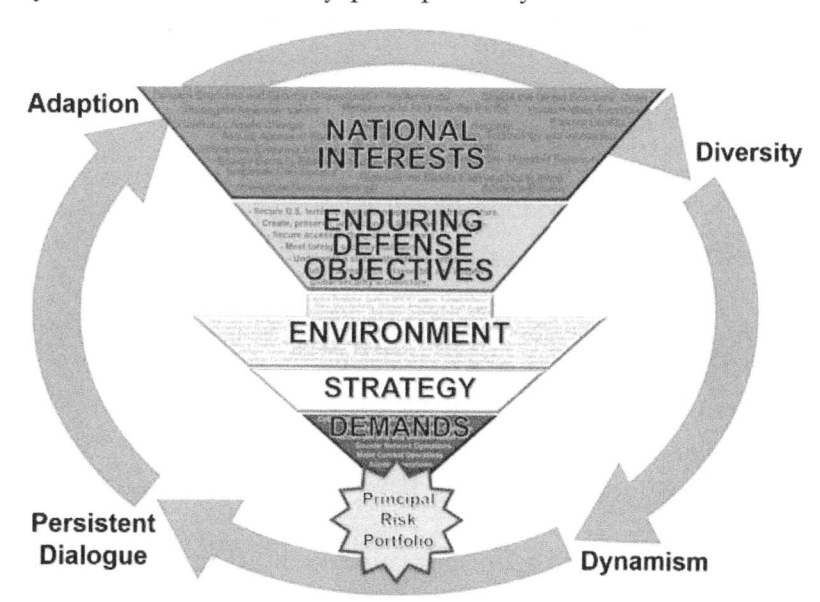

Figure VI-1. Four Governing Principles of Post Primacy Risk.

As was suggested above, DoD faces a daunting collection of diverse and dynamic challenges that do not always conform well to extant U.S./partner defense convention. These challenges are also changing or metastasizing well within the turning radius of traditional U.S./partner defense and national security bureaucracies.[4] Thus, **adaptation**—as conceived here—includes risk avoidance, acceptance, transfer, and mitigation. However, it further hints at the requirement for more radical enterprise-level innovation, as well when risk judgments warrant it. Given the evolution—or more accurately revolution and devolution—in international security conditions, more fundamental risk-driven **adaptation** may be essential to restore or maintain U.S. competitive advantages, freedom of action, and strategic options.

DIVERSITY AND DYNAMISM—THE PRINCIPAL RISK PORTFOLIO

The most obvious exemplar of this study's belief in a new, more adaptable postprimacy risk concept is the idea of a principal risk portfolio. Through the course of the research effort, the USAWC study team concluded that the aperture through which DoD identified risk was too narrow. Instead of a thoroughgoing survey of the consequential hazards paired to enduring defense objectives, DoD currently opts for a simple five hazard construction against which it forges global strategy and assesses the risk associated with that strategy's successful prosecution. Because current strategy and risk assessment are firmly pegged exclusively to near-term traditional military threats, they leave a conceptual space between, above, and below these hazards. Moreover, this space is the likeliest source of near-, mid-, and long-term surprise, shock, failure, and prohibitive cost.

While surge demand was or is the coin of the realm in risk assessment, current defense convention limits the concept of surge to its most conservative interpretations. Current surge considerations for DoD largely revolve around the major commitment of U.S. capabilities in high-end combined arms warfighting, as well as in support of the contemporary counterterrorism challenge. Note that DoD captures the five hazards in a strategy, planning, and risk assessment tool or model commonly identified as the "4 plus 1."[5]

The "4 plus 1" is a traditional threat-based construction of defense priorities, grounded in post-9/11 realism. It is a living embodiment of corporate convention and bias. The "4," for example, predictably represent the traditional military hazards and U.S. responses to China, Russia, Iran, and North Korea. The "1," on the other hand, captures both the hazards and defense responsibilities having to do with violent Islamic extremism.

Both the study team and the vast majority of those stakeholders engaged over the course of the research effort found the "4 plus 1" construction to be an inadequate instrument for identifying compelling risks at the strategic and military levels of analysis. Instead, with the near-consensus support of risk-interested stakeholders and analysts, this study found that the pacing concept for fulsome **strategic** and **military risk** begins with an examination of the relationship between the contemporary decision-making environment, at-risk enduring defense objectives (embedded in a coherent defense strategy), the most compelling hazards to those objectives emerging from the environment, and the surge demands associated with securing or defending those at-risk objectives. A short-hand description of this would be an objective-based vice threat-based approach to risk assessment.

The team concluded that identification of the generic defense demands tied directly to the security of enduring defense objectives was the first critical component of a new, more diverse and dynamic risk and risk assessment concept. **Diversity** in the consideration of hazards and responses must by definition stretch conventional wisdom and inherent defense bias. Thus, the principle of a more **diverse** risk assessment process argues against measuring and remeasuring the "known knowns" alone on a cyclical basis.[6] From the study team's vantage point, this appears to be the current norm. The trite truism that DoD has a perfect record in its failure to predict the next major conflict or contingency is inspiration enough to widen the risk aperture to account for a broader set of demands than current risk convention entertains.[7]

This was in fact one of the earliest insights to emerge from the study team's work. The team determined that it would employ the concepts of **importance** and **urgency** first to identify pacing defense demands that should be included in a new principal risk portfolio. The team concluded that the principal risk portfolio should include all surge demands (and associated capabilities and capacity) essential to securing DoD's enduring defense objectives over the next decade. Doing so ensures that senior leaders have the most complete risk picture to inform their major strategic choices.

As was outlined in Section III, **importance** implies judgments as to an individual demand's criticality to the defense or security of one or more at-risk enduring defense objectives. It marries current Pentagon conceptions of "strength of interest" and measurable adverse "consequences."[8] The most important surge demands are those that have the greatest material impact on either the most significant and/or the greatest number of enduring defense objectives. Senior leader judgements on **importance** answer the simple question: "Where does this demand sit in priority in relation to other significant defense responsibilities?"

Urgency, on the other hand, involves judgments on the extent and timing of required action. It is fundamentally informed or shaped by high-level perspectives on the need or pressure to employ or prepare for a specific surge demand. The most urgent demands require action now to actively meet specific contingency requirements or address dangerous future vulnerabilities that will manifest in profoundly consequential ways.

At its core, **urgency** involves time-dependent judgments related to when senior leadership believe a particular demand will be either most operative or most vulnerable to failure or fatal weakness. Again, employing some common Pentagon risk language, **urgency** is the marriage of a hazard's likelihood with the velocity of its emergence, its rate of change or adaptation, and the perceived time senior U.S. leaders have to respond to it effectively.

Again, while Section III introduces the basics of the principal risk portfolio, additional key insights about it bear repeating here. For example, in addition to **importance** and **urgency**, construction of and insights related to the principal risk portfolio rely on senior-level judgments in two further areas. These are **capability/capacity**, and **agility**.

The former—**capability/capacity**—involves judgments on the degree to which the U.S. defense enterprise is or is not missioned, manned, equipped (conceptually and materially), and postured to meet identified surge demands. It is in short an aggregate judgment on near-, mid-, and long-term readiness for the specific demands articulated in the principal risk portfolio. The **capability** side of this single consideration ponders the question: "Are we materially and conceptually ready for this type of demand?" Considerations of **capacity**, on the other hand, involve judgments on an anticipated demand's scope, scale, and duration matched against the postulated extent or limits of anticipated U.S. responses (e.g., breadth, depth, and endurance of U.S. forces and capabilities). With respect to **capacity**, the more operative questions are: "Are we ready for demands of this size and, if so, for how long?"

The last concept—**agility**—involves senior-level judgments on the degree to which DoD can or is anticipated to be able to flex resources, innovate, and adapt to the unique requirements of a particular demand, whether or not pre-existing **capability/capacity** is present. **Agility** is more than the ability to swing resources to new challenges. Instead, it is in fact an aggregate view of DoD's ability to both redirect resources and adapt strategy, plans, capabilities, and concepts to meet unanticipated or under-anticipated demands. The critical question on the subject of **agility** is: "Are DoD's human and material resources deft enough to adjust to relatively sudden or unexpected changes in defense priorities within and from outside the principal risk portfolio?"

Side-by-side comparison of these four characteristics as they relate to the portfolio and specific manifestations of defense demand assist senior leadership in identifying obvious U.S./partner strengths, potential vulnerabilities, as well as particularly salient points of strategic uncertainty. The next section of this study outlines an illustration of the principal risk portfolio in practice in order to demonstrate these points.

THE PRINCIPAL RISK PORTFOLIO IN PRACTICE

The authors suggest that the principal risk portfolio provides DoD strategy and risk assessment with an aim point that more realistically and meaningfully represents the inherent **diversity** and **dynamism** of 21st-century defense demand. The study's emphasis on identifying unique demands and employing them in a portfolio approach to risk assessment argues against pacing DoD strategy and risk assessment to confront either specific near-term threats or one to two archetypal military demands (e.g., major theater war and counterterrorism). Neither approach effectively encourages the requisite degree of institutional **adaptation** essential to confront post-primacy conditions.

Further, the team would argue that the latter two perspectives hazard missing the sudden or unexpected onset of either an entirely different set of important and/or urgent demands or unexpected, radical reordering of defense priorities. Both could overwhelm DoD's response **capability**, **capacity**, and **agility**.

Risk assessment in relation to specific near-term military demands is already embedded in the annual process of risk assessment currently led by the Chairman of the Joint Chiefs of Staff (CJCS).[9] The process likely should remain intact, as it is currently an adequate measure of near-term military readiness. However, it likely should not be the final determinant of enterprise-level **strategic** and **military risk**. This report argues for a more fulsome and persistent near-, mid-, and long-term corporate risk assessment **dialogue** that looks at the two key axes of **strategic/military** and **operational/future challenges risk** and is based on an objectives-driven portfolio approach. In the study team's view, this approach will render clearer risk insights for DoD with respect to contending with and balancing immediate requirements while deliberately adapting overtime to evolutionary and revolutionary future demands.

Construction of the illustrative principal risk portfolio began with an analysis of the national security and defense strategy policy dating back to the first Bush administration. This effort resulted in identification of the enduring defense objectives already referenced throughout the report. As was pointed out in Section III and IV, the report's consumers will recognize the objectives as fairly consistent 25-year features of U.S. policy and strategy.

The next step saw the study team identify the dominant features of DoD's 10-year decision-making environment, as well as that environment's current and forecasted hazards. In addition, as the project was getting underway and to gain insights on what important and urgent contemporary demand looked like, the study team surveyed a broad cross-section of DoD and defense analysis professionals to determine their "top five" potential surge demands over the next decade.[10] A graphic depiction of the results of that survey and the associated demands can be found in Appendix I of this report.

As expected, this effort generated a sizable list of plausible defense-relevant concerns. Many reflected the specific responsibilities of the respondents. However, all consistently communicated hazards presenting meaningful challenges to enduring defense objectives.

Acknowledging that it was both unnecessary and impossible to develop and sustain capabilities and capacity targeted at each individual concern, the study team synthesized the various responses, contextualized them within the posited decision-making environment, compared them to the proposed set of **enduring defense objectives**, and binned them into common demand typologies. That process yielded eight illustrative 10-year surge demands. Together, these eight pacing demands comprise the study's illustrative principal risk portfolio, they include:
- Strategic Deterrence and Defense;
- Gray Zone/Counter-Gray Zone;
- Access/Anti-Access;
- Major Combat;
- Distributed Security;[11]
- Influence and Counter-Influence;
- Counter-Network;[12] and,
- Humanitarian Assistance and Consequence Management.[13]

Table VI-1 provides a working description of each surge demand.

The team believes these eight demands (or something like them), combined into a portfolio of prioritized defense concerns, should be a start point for pacing DoD strategy and risk assessment over the next decade. Persistent risk assessment may see pacing demands rise and fall in priority or be supplanted by new important and urgent requirements. Thus, the team suggests these begin but do not end a more fulsome 21st-century risk **dialogue**.

Illustrative Surge Demand	Description
Strategic Deterrence and Defense	Military activities, operations, or campaigns associated with securing the air, sea, space, maritime and cyber sovereignty of the United States and deterring or defeating aggression against the United States with weapons of mass destruction (most prominently nuclear weapons).
Gray Zone/Counter-Gray Zone	Military activities, operations, or campaigns associated with employing or defeating "gray zone" approaches to competition and conflict.
Access/Anti-Access	Military activities, operations, or campaigns associated with gaining and maintaining access to contested space or denying access to the same.
Major Combat	Military activities, operations, or campaigns associated with large-scale employment of traditional combined arms capability against a competitor's traditional military forces.
Distributed Security	Military activities, operations, or campaigns associated with defeating irregular adversaries and/or "gaining control over and securing geography, infrastructure, populations, or dangerous military capabilities threatened by . . . disorder."[14]
Influence/Counter-Influence	Military activities, operations, or campaigns associated with employing or countering non-lethal information-based assets to achieve distinct politico-security outcomes.
Counter-Network	Military activities, operations, or campaigns associated with "systematically disrupting or dismantling hostile nonstate networks."[15]
Humanitarian Assistance and Consequence Management	Military activities, operations, or campaigns associated with "temporarily reliev[ing] human suffering, provid[ing] basic public goods, and help[ing] offset immediate threats to public safety and health in the wake of catastrophe or domestic disasters."[16]

Table VI-1. Illustrative 10-Year Surge Demands and Their Descriptions.

The eight demands do not represent the sum total of activity in specific military operations or campaigns but, rather, their prevailing character. For example, there may be significant high-intensity combat in a future "distributed security" scenario. Nonetheless, its overall character remains defeating irregular adversaries and/or "gaining control over and securing geography, infrastructure, populations, or dangerous military capabilities threatened by foreign disorder."[17] Further, Russian aggression toward NATO-member states, Iranian regional hybrid warfare activities, and China's campaign to expand its control over the South China Sea all exemplify physiognomies of gray zone operations and attendant American responsibility for developing effective gray zone counters to them.

As suggested, the surge demands are evaluated within the portfolio in light of four key concepts—**importance**, **urgency**, **capability/capacity**, and finally, perceived U.S./partner **agility**. While the portfolio is perceived as inclusive of all the demands necessary to secure at-risk enduring defense objectives, the demands of most concern to senior leaders should be those exhibiting considerable asymmetry between **urgency** and **importance** on the one hand and **capability**, **capacity**, and **agility** on the other.

All of the demands that made the initial cut for this illustrative portfolio are considered **important** and **urgent** in gross terms. However, that initial cut then requires a more thorough assessment of both **importance** and **urgency** compared to one another, as well as DoD's inherent **capability**, **capacity**, and **agility** to deal with each in the most appropriate and effective manner possible. Some demands therefore are **important** but less **urgent**. Some are **urgent** but less **important**. Finally, some might be very **important** and **urgent,** but are substantially lacking the **capability**, **capacity**, or **agility** essential to meeting their unique requirements and successfully securing **enduring defense objectives**.

Figure VI-2 represents this report's illustrative portfolio and relevant study team judgments on **importance**, **urgency**, **capability/capacity**, and **agility**. It is intended to demonstrate the utility of the portfolio approach. A simple thought exercise demonstrates the point.

Note that "Major Combat" is identified as among the most important challenges depicted, yet it is also considered only moderately urgent. Further, it also boasts significant pre-existing **capability** and **capacity** but, from the study team's perspective, benefits from only moderate **agility**. Likewise, in the study team's judgment, "Gray Zone/Counter-Gray Zone" is considered very important and urgent, but nonetheless exhibits significant shortcomings in both **capability/capacity** and **agility**. The portfolio and senior judgments on **importance**, **urgency**, **capability/capacity**, and **agility** generate significant risk insights by themselves.

The study team suggests that use of a decision tool like the principal risk portfolio offers senior defense leaders with opportunities for a more frank, candid, and straightforward appreciation of the range or **diversity of important** and **urgent** 21st-century defense demands. Indeed, one senior review group (SRG) participant suggested the portfolio by itself would be immensely useful for structuring senior-level risk discussions.[18] The portfolio further enables meaningful consideration by DoD's leadership of how both hazards and their associated demands can and will change over time. More on this subject follows in the next few sections.

The study team argues that the portfolio approach forces consideration of a much more representative sample of near-, mid-, and long-term defense requirements. It further provides senior leadership with an adaptable tool that enables a meaningful risk-based discussion of both DoD's principal focus and azimuth (**strategic risk**), as well as its near-, mid-, and long-term readiness for discrete military demands (**military risk**). Anything less invites significant "hidden risk."[19]

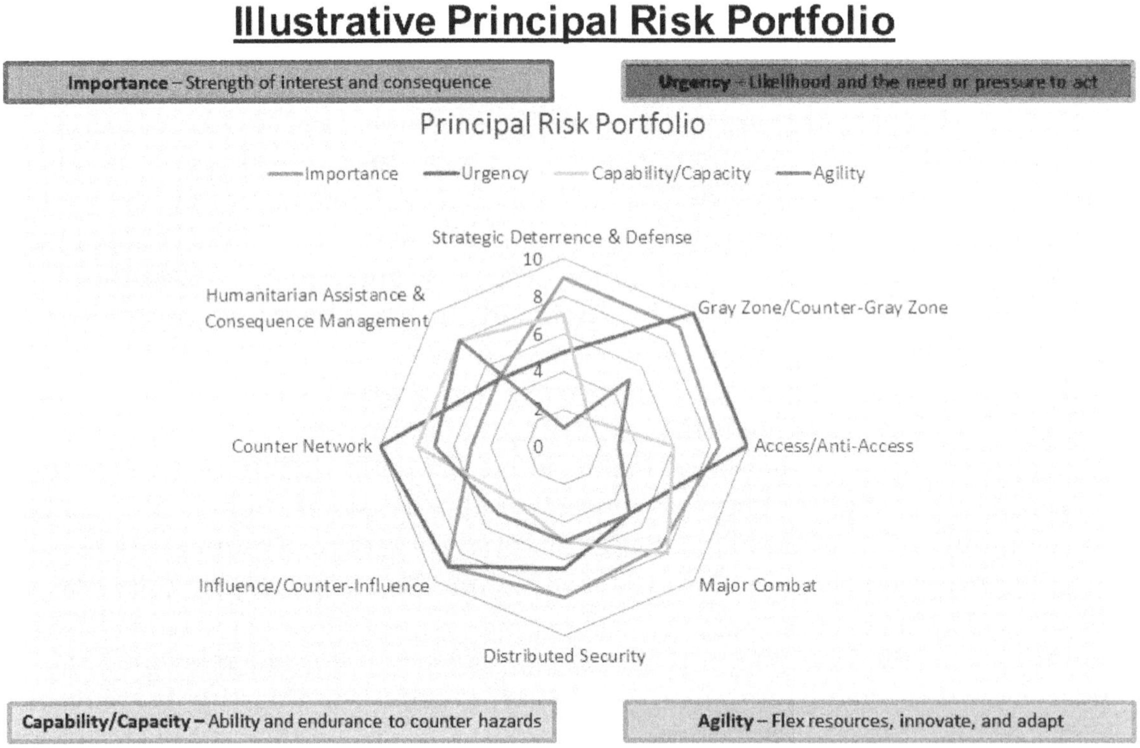

Illustrative Principal Risk Portfolio

Figure VI-2. Illustrative Principal Risk Portfolio.

CHANGE AS CONSTANT: DYNAMISM IN THE NATURE OF HAZARD AND RESPONSE

Dynamism is naturally embedded in the principal risk portfolio concept. Yet, a separate detailed discussion of **dynamism** as a foundational concept for future DoD risk assessment is warranted here.

Over the course of the study effort, the team found that most risk assessments were static snapshots in time. Current assessments of operational risk, for example, only tell senior leadership about the near-term hazards associated with particular plans.[21] This study suggests that the likelihood of DoD being asked to unexpectedly go "off-script" remains very high. This is particularly true in light of the five characteristics of the post-primacy environment outlined in Section V. Therefore, a

> *Over the long term, we face the risk of uncertainty inherent to the dynamic nature of the security environment. Although the Joint Force will gradually become more modern, we will face risks as others develop and field advanced capabilities and sophisticated weapons systems. We will have less margin of error to deal with unforeseen shifts in the security environment.*[20]

constant search for change in strategic circumstances must be a bedrock of meaningful 21st-century risk assessment.

In a word, the environment is marked by a degree of **dynamism** that now certainly outpaces the evaluative and decision-making **capability** of extant military bureaucracy. In short, DoD is a mid-20th-century institution struggling to keep pace with devolution of the post-Cold War status quo and a security environment defined by diverse and dynamic challenges prone to both metastasis and metamorphosis.

Both the dead space between military/strategic and operational/future challenges risk, as well as the inherent **dynamism** or movement of hazards and responses up and down the scales of **urgency** and **importance,** are for the most part lost in the current art of DoD risk assessment. If one accepts the principal risk portfolio as an organizing approach, it too could be prone to harbor miscalculation unless DoD commits to a persistent program of risk assessment that constantly monitors changes in strategic circumstances and adjusts risk judgments accordingly.

Thus, this study concludes that recognition of the inherent **dynamism** or change in the type or character of hazards requiring surges in DoD demand over time is an essential standard for effective risk calculation. Likewise, the study team acknowledges that there is substantial **dynamism** in U.S./partner **capability**, **capacity**, and readiness over time as well. Therefore, to the extent possible, senior DoD leadership must maintain an unblinking eye on the constant change occurring on all sides of the contemporary defense equation.

PERSISTENT DIALOGUE: SIX CRITICAL RISK CONSIDERATIONS

In consultation with key stakeholders, as well as the expert working group (EWG) and SRG, the USAWC study team concluded that wherever a contemporary DoD risk convention or concept was evident, it was in fact too mechanical or formulaic to yield practical or meaningful post-primacy insights over the **near-**, **mid-**, and **long-**term. Further, it may be less useful in gauging the overall orientation and direction of DoD strategy and planning over the same time horizon. According to one veteran service representative participating in the study's EWG, "Americans will always try to apply method to art. Assessing strategic and military risk will defy method and quantification."[22] In brief, current convention likely does not fully examine risk along the two critical axes identified in this report—**military/strategic** and **operational/future challenges**.

As argued, the Chairman's Risk Assessment (CRA) is a useful process for examining the risks associated with the known knowns of current theater-level plans. However, it is likely a less effective tool for gauging the near-, mid-, and long-term evolution in defense hazards that invariably interrupt the rhythm of contemporary defense and military convention. Accepting that **diversity** and **dynamism** are the first two governing principles for post-primacy risk assessment, this study found that the most

> *We have seen a tendency to separate risks into rigid silos—operational risk, market risk, credit risk and so on. . . . But what we have found is that major shocks and problems do not come that way. . . . unless you have an integrated view of risk, you could encounter major problems.*[23]

effective route to meaningful **strategic** and **military risk** insights at the enterprise-level runs through a third governing concept involving persistent, structured, and strategy-focused **dialogue** among DoD's senior leadership.

79

Indeed, both the focus and persistence of this dialogue on the most important aspects of defense strategy make it the centerpiece of any post-primacy risk assessment concept. According to an unpublished paper by U.S. Special Operations Command (USSOCOM), "Periodic assessments of risk are insufficient; risk management must be embedded in routine organizational processes and requires senior leader involvement."[24]

The **dialogue** begins with a clear understanding of the principal risk portfolio, as well as an appreciation for how it and **important** and **urgent** objectives and hazards might evolve over time. The portfolio is the fruit of a deeper understanding of the relationship between at-risk enduring defense objectives, consequential hazards, prospective surge defense demands, and the defense priorities they all suggest. After identifying the portfolio and its constituent demands, the next natural step in corporate risk assessment must be a persistent enterprise-level **dialogue** focused on a finite set of core considerations. These considerations address key near-, mid-, and long-term questions revolving around issues including but not limited to:

- The ability of DoD to attend to multiple simultaneous demands;
- Future demands around which a **capability** or **capacity** have yet to mature;
- Demands whose environmental change vector indicates that our current **capability/capacity** may be insufficient given circumstances; or finally,
- Anticipated demands where U.S. advantage or leverage is in doubt.

Given the hyper-competitive nature of DoD's contemporary decision-making environment, there is a single dominant risk consideration for senior defense leadership in this dialogue. It is the degree or extent of leverage or advantage that U.S. decision-makers hold over either the environment overall or specific defense-relevant strategic circumstances or challenges they anticipate confronting. The dialogue should involve a 360-degree discussion involving red, blue, green, gray, and black considerations. According to Mackenzie Eaglen of the American Enterprise Institute, risk is all about this leverage or what she describes as "military balance":

> [M]ilitary risk includes the length of time it takes to win; the number of casualties [expected]; outright mission failure, and a qualitative and quantitative assessment of the military balance [or leverage] relative to our enemy . . . A holistic appreciation of strategic risk should also include . . . a heavy emphasis on the relative military balance [or leverage] over time.[25]

The study identified six other important considerations for senior DoD leadership as they assess their relative leverage or advantage in the context of a new or adapted post-primacy risk concept. Combined with leverage or advantage the following six considerations draw insights from the **diversity** and **dynamism** of the principal risk portfolio and are building blocks of the very kind of persistent, structured strategy-focused **risk assessment concept** demanded by a decision-making environment fraught with constant, consequential change.

The first consideration is a meaningful discussion of **the nature, clarity, and origin of near-, mid-, and long-term defense challenges and their relationship to current U.S./partner conventions, strategy, plans, and priorities**. Success here hinges on honest self-appraisal at senior levels of DoD about its corporate understanding of and response to high-level evolution or revolution in the defense and security landscape over time. It asks and answers foundational questions about trends in the environment like those outlined in Section V. This consideration addresses the principal orientation and primary motives of defense strategy both as a whole and in its more basic components. Insights derived here would be more fulsome if combined with similar perspectives from sister ministries of defense and defense-interested quarters of the U.S. Government (e.g., the White House, the Departments of State and Homeland Security, and the intelligence community).

A second critical consideration is deep understanding of **the residual or hidden risks impacting defense challenges and prior U.S./partner approaches to mitigating, accepting, transferring, or avoiding them**. This study's 9-month survey of defense communities of interest and practice (including the EWG and SRG) found risk to be a compounding quality in defense and military affairs. Nonetheless, there was rarely any retrospective appraisal within DoD of how past risk accumulated to create hidden or under-appreciated military- or strategic-level peril. According one senior service leader, "We don't know how much risk we are carrying" at any given time.[26] Consequently, this latent risk is rarely accounted for in strategy development and strategic forecasting or planning.[27] This study suggests that this consideration remain central to any enterprise-level risk **dialogue**.

The character, complexity, rate of change, and endurance of defense challenges and perceived U.S./partner competency, anticipation, adaptability, depth, and resilience account for the same. This third key consideration in a persistent, well-structured **dialogue** on corporate-level risk draws on the insights of the previous two. It seeks to help DoD understand how the institution, its components, and its principal allies and partners anticipate and respond to change in strategic circumstances. It answers very basic questions about how well the U.S. defense instrument is prepared to succeed in the face of an environment prone to persistent metamorphosis and metastasis.[28] It asks senior-level defense and military leadership to persistently and honestly appraise DoD's fitness for a diverse and dynamic demand portfolio and the likelihood that uncertainty (with its propensity for surprise and shock) is the only certainty in contemporary defense strategy and planning.

The fourth and fifth considerations are tightly connected. The fourth is **the scope, scale, and diversity of defense challenges and presumed U.S./partner capacity to absorb their attendant requirements**. The fifth consideration is **the spatial and temporal sequencing of the defense challenges and presumed U.S./partner responsiveness, reach, and flexibility**. They address separate, but nonetheless related questions. In the first instance—scope, scale, and **diversity**—the issue at hand is: what kind of defense demands and to what extent will they manifest over time? Whereas the latter consideration examines where and when hazards will materialize in the near-, mid-, and long-terms. In response, senior defense and military leadership must assess the degree or extent to which they cover down on the broad front of challenges they may encounter and when and where they should be prepared to reach out to contend with them.

Finally, in light of all the insights gathered in a meaningful risk dialogue, senior defense and military leadership are charged with making **overall judgments on existing or prospective U.S./partner defense leverage (or advantage) vis-à-vis defense challenges, as well as identification of available U.S./partner opportunities**. The discussion of the six considerations began with this important idea of advantage or leverage. In the final analysis, determination of the extent to which the United States and its defense instrument exercise leverage or advantage vis-à-vis individual or collective defense hazards is the quintessential question prior to making final risk management judgments. More leverage or demonstrable advantage is obviously better. However, senior defense leadership cannot ignore opportunities or current and future competitive advantages that may in fact reduce or eliminate risk that has not yet fully materialized but is nonetheless anticipated.[29]

Employment of these basic considerations in a holistic enterprise-level **dialogue** allows for a high-level, deliberate, and sophisticated appraisal of the near-, mid-, and long-term risks associated with a defense strategy and its implementation over time. Together they are less a checklist and more an agenda. Each individually weighs both exogenous and endogenous conditions to arrive at key insights relative to defense strategy and planning. These insights arm senior defense and military leaders with an uncomplicated but not unsophisticated risk picture against which they can then weigh and make the most important choices at the **military** and **strategic** levels of analysis.

Further, these considerations can be applied against extant military plans or concepts, long operative at the center of DoD's decision-making. Likewise, they can project U.S./partner risk as it applies to prospective contingency circumstances that are forecasted but currently not well-considered in defense strategy and planning. Finally, they stand ready for rapid employment against true "black swans" that emerge from sudden unanticipated change in strategic conditions.[30]

ADAPT (OR PERISH?)

A late but critical insight emerging from the USAWC study effort concerned the symbiotic relationship between risk assessment and enterprise-level defense **adaptation**.[31] The study team discovered a significant concern among key stakeholders is that current DoD risk convention and urgent defense **adaptation** had in fact become de-linked.[32] Of course, there is some evidence to the contrary. One can argue, for example, that initiatives like the "third offset" or "air-sea battle" are or were risk-driven strategic choices by senior DoD leadership.[33]

However, given the velocity and nature of change in strategic circumstances, this insight does harbor the potential for profound vulnerability and, therefore, merits significant attention by senior DoD leadership going forward. Inspired by genuine stakeholder concern, the USAWC study team asked and answered a very simple and important question on the subject of risk and **adaptation**: Does current risk convention encourage effective defense **adaptation** by being sufficiently comprehensive, agile, and forward-looking? In the end, given the insights generated throughout the research effort, this study concludes that it is not on all counts. And, in response, the study suggests that the principles of **diversity**, **dynamism**, and persistent (and sophisticated) **dialogue** will — if employed aggressively — result in risk insights that at a minimum suggest areas of meaningful **adaptation**.

Adaptation in this regard is more than just a "buzz word." It includes effective near-term adjustment to adversary innovation and changes in threat profile. In addition, as importantly and under current post-primacy conditions, it must also be by definition far more forward-leaning and anticipatory.[34] Thus, the types of **adaptations** implied in risk judgments will range from discrete changes to near-term concepts of operation to and through a more fundamental reordering of future defense priorities, recalibration of important defense capabilities, and re-missioning of military forces.

The study team suggests that a senior-level risk identification and assessment process guided by the four governing principles, outlined earlier, will yield far more significant and ground-breaking insights than current convention might allow. Moreover, consequently, it will inform and drive more effective post-primacy defense strategy and planning. Section VIII describes how defense and military leaders might use the four governing principles and the six critical risk considerations to effectively communicate hazard and response both to themselves and to those outside of DoD most concerned with DoD's risk-based choices.

ENDNOTES – SECTION VI

1. National Intelligence Council, *Global Trends: Paradox of Progress*, Washington, DC: National Intelligence Council, January 9, 2017, p. ix, available from *https://www.dni.gov/index.php/global-trends-home*, accessed January 14, 2017.

2. See the 2010 *Quadrennial Defense Review* (QDR) and Chairman of the Joint Chiefs of Staff Manual (CJCSM) 3105.01 for defense descriptions and definitions of **operational risk** and **future challenges** risk. Robert Gates, *Quadrennial Defense Review Report*, Washington, DC: U.S. Department of Defense, February 2010, p. 118, available from *history.defense.gov/Historical-Sources/Quadrennial-Defense-Review/*, accessed May 4, 2017; Chairman of the Joint Chiefs of Staff (CJCS), CJCSM 3105.01, *Joint Risk Analysis*, Washington, DC: U.S. Department of Defense, October 14, 2016, pp. C8-C9, available from *www.jcs.mil/Library/CJCS-Manuals/*, accessed February 2, 2017.

3. National Intelligence Council, pp. 17, 19, 179-181, 209. This report offers myriad insights on the impact of rapid technological change.

4. This insight was derived from a detailed conversation with working-level Joint Staff strategists at the Pentagon, Washington, DC, February 17, 2017.

5. Colin Clark, "CJCS Dunford Calls For Strategic Shifts; 'At Peace Or At War Is Insufficient'," Breaking Defense, September 21, 2016, available from *breakingdefense.com/2016/09/cjcs-dunford-calls-for-strategic-shifts-at-peace-or-at-war-is-insufficient/*, accessed May 13, 2017.

6. See for example John P. Girard and JoAnn L. Girard, *A Leader's Guide to Knowledge Management: Drawing on the Past to Enhance Future Performance*, New York: Business Expert Press, 2009, pp. 54-55. The phrase "known, knowns" is attributable to former Secretary of Defense Donald Rumsfeld who made the now famous remarks during a February 12, 2002, Pentagon press conference, explaining:

> Reports that say that something hasn't happened are always interesting to me, because as we know, there are known knowns; there are things we know we know. We also know there are known unknowns; that is to say we know there are some things we do not know. But there are also unknown unknowns—the ones we don't know we don't know. And if one looks throughout the history of our country and other free countries, it is the latter category that tend to be the difficult ones.

The full transcript is available from *archive.defense.gov/Transcripts/Transcript.aspx?TranscriptID=2636*, accessed May 13, 2017. The book, *A Leader's Guide*, discusses the remarks and illustrates how Secretary Rumsfeld "very concisely described a major complex management challenge."

7. "Text of Secretary of Defense Robert Gates' Feb. 25, 2011, speech at West Point," *Stars and Strips*, February 27, 2011, available from *https://www.stripes.com/news/text-of-secretary-of-defense-robert-gates-feb-25-2011-speech-at-west-point-1.136145#.WRYA0mtMTct*, accessed May 12, 2017.

8. CJCS, CJCSM 3105.01, p. C-4.

9. *Ibid.*

10. The study team asked for response to 4 questions: How would you characterize strategic-level "military risk"? What are the principal components of strategic-level "military risk"? What do you perceive to be the Department of Defense's (DoD) Top 5 "surge" military demands between 2017-2027? and finally, What are the "building blocks" that constitute your view of steady state military demand from 2017-2027?

11. Nathan Freier, proj. dir., David Berteau, prog. dir., Stephanie Sanok, Jacquelyn Guy, Curtis Buzzard, Errol Laumann, Steven Nicolucci, J.P. Pellegrino, Sam Eaton, and Megan Loney, cont. auths., *Beyond the Last War: Balancing Ground Forces and Future Challenges Risk in USCENTCOM and USPACOM*, Washington, DC: Center for Strategic and International Studies, 2013, p. IX.

12. *Ibid.*

13. *Ibid.* p. 6.

14. *Ibid.*, p. IX.

15. Nathan Freier, pri. auth., Daniel Bilko, Matthew Driscoll, Akhil Iyer, Walter Rugen, Terrence Smith, Matthew Trollinger, cont. auths., Maren Leed, proj. dir., *U.S. Ground Force Capabilities Through 2020*, Washington, DC: Center for Strategic and International Studies, October 2011, p. 3.

16. Freier *et al.*, *Beyond the Last War*, p. 6.

17. *Ibid.*, p. IX.

18. Comment of former senior Joint Staff officer who participated in the senior review group (SRG) discussion at National Defense University, Washington, DC, March 30, 2017.

19. *Ibid.*

20. Chuck Hagel, *Quadrennial Defense Review 2014*, Washington, DC: U.S. Department of Defense, March 2014, p. 39, available from *archive.defense.gov/pubs/2014_Quadrennial_Defense_Review.pdf*, accessed May 3, 2017.

21. This insight emerged from the expert working group (EWG) discussion that occurred at National Defense University, Washington, DC, November 16, 2016. It was confirmed through multiple interactions with Combatant Command-level stakeholders on January 17, 2017.

22. This insight was provided to the study team via an emailed survey response from an EWG member on August 10, 2017.

23. Wharton economist, Richard J. Herring, Ph.D., quoted in "Re-thinking Risk Management: Why the Mindset Matters More Than the Model," Knowledge@Wharton, April 15, 2009, available from *knowledge.wharton.upenn.edu/article/re-thinking-risk-management-why-the-mindset-matters-more-than-the-model/*, accessed May 5, 2017.

24. U.S. Special Operations Command (USSOCOM), "Risk Concept Paper," unpublished staff paper provided to the study team on a visit to USSOCOM headquarters at MacDill Air Force Base, FL, January 17, 2017, p. 1.

25. Survey response received via email from Mackenzie Eaglen of the American Enterprise Institute.

26. This quoted insight came from a senior service representative during consultations at the Pentagon, Washington, DC, April 11, 2017.

27. This insight is the product of multiple encounters with defense-interested practitioners and thought leaders throughout the course of the study effort. It was reinforced during consultation with a senior service representative at the Pentagon, Washington, DC, April 11, 2017.

28. See for example T.X. Hammes, "The Future of Conflict," in R. D. Hooker, Jr., ed., *Charting a Course: Strategic Choices for a New Administration*, Washington, DC: NDU Press, December 12, 2016, available from *ndupress.ndu.edu/Publications/Books/charting-a-course/Article/1026964/chapter-2-the-future-of-conflict/*, accessed May 13, 2017. The author asserts that the changing character of war is continuous and demands constant adaptation to the way the United States must prepare for war. He further asserts, "Despite assertions to the contrary, war is not disappearing. If anything, it is increasing in frequency and duration. Armed conflict will remain central to relations among states and nonstate actors." Another example is offered by Andrew F. Krepinevich, "Alternative Approaches to Defense Strategy," Senate Armed Services Committee Testimony, October 30, 2015, available from *csbaonline.org/research/publications/alternative-approaches-to-defense-strategy/publication*, accessed May 13, 2017. The author describes changing U.S. strategy, national security resourcing, and the rise of revisionist powers like Russia, China, and Iran, explaining that, "Together, these developments have greatly increased the scale of the security challenges confronting the United States relative to what they were less than a decade ago."

29. An EWG member raised and advocated for injecting more positive impacts or competitive advantages into the risk assessment process during deliberations at the National Defense University, Washington, DC, November 5, 2016. The study team agreed and included it here.

30. For a discussion/definition of "black swans" see Nassim Nicholas Taleb, *The Black Swan: The Impact of the Highly Improbable*, New York: Random House, 2007.

31. Insights on adaptation and its central role in missioning the risk assessment process emerged from repeated consultations with representatives of the Joint Staff during multiple engagements in Washington, DC, over the course of the study.

32. This insight was derived from a detailed conversation with working-level Joint Staff strategists at the Pentagon, Washington, DC, February 17, 2017, and was confirmed during consultations with the senior review group at National Defense University, Washington, DC, March 30, 2017.

33. For an overview of these concepts see, Cheryl Pellerin, "Deputy Secretary: Third Offset Strategy Bolsters America's Military Deterrence," DoD News, October 31, 2016, available from *https://www.defense.gov/News/Article/Article/991434/deputy-secretary-third-offset-strategy-bolsters-americas-military-deterrence*, accessed April 4, 2017; Department of Defense Air-Sea Battle Office, "Air-Sea Battle: Service Collaboration to Address Anti-Access & Area Denial Challenges," Washington, DC, U.S. Department of Defense, May 2013, available from *archive.defense.gov/pubs/ASB-ConceptImplementation-Summary-May-2013.pdf*, accessed April 4, 2017.

34. The idea of anticipatory adaptation was highlighted in a written response from one member of the senior review group received via email on March 30, 2017.

VII. COMMUNICATING RISK: A COMMON RISK CURRENCY

Communication has always been an imperfect science, reliant on a common appreciation of the meaning, implication and tone of language being used. Misinterpretation of messages will impact the performance of even the simplest of corporate entities.[1]

Among many objectives, this report attempts to offer senior defense and military leadership a common risk currency—or as Andy Bulgin suggests, a "common appreciation of meaning"—that it might employ to describe, identify, assess, and communicate key risk insights. The currency is meant for use both within the Pentagon, as well as outside of the Department of Defense (DoD) in forums requiring that defense and military leadership communicate effectively with high-impact constituencies most interested in DoD's risk-based strategic choices. These constituencies include the White House and Capitol Hill, as well as the defense analysis community, opinion-makers, and the broader general public.

> *Precision of communication is important, more important than ever, in our era of hair trigger balances, when a false or misunderstood word may create as much disaster as a sudden thoughtless act.*[2]

This report suggests that wide acceptance of a new common risk currency begins with clear understanding of the principles of **diversity, dynamism, persistent dialogue,** and **adaptation** across DoD, its service components and agencies, and its functional and theater-level commands. One senior service representative engaged in the course of this study suggested that all involved in the current risk **dialogue** were "numb" to the subject.[3] This suggests that there needs to be some change not only in how DoD assesses risk but also in how it communicates it, both within and outside of the Pentagon.

This report is largely dedicated to the former. Here the study team briefly addresses the latter. In straightforward terms, the study team suggests the simple parsimonious principles of **diversity, dynamism, persistent dialogue,** and **adaptation** offer new opportunities for defense senior leaders to communicate meaningful risk insights through an uncomplicated but not unsophisticated construction. Naturally, use of this format must be preceded by clear and unambiguous articulation of enduring defense objectives, important and urgent hazards, surge demands, and adopted or proposed strategic courses of action. These are stage-setting terms of reference for the wider risk discussion that follows.

Preceding articulation of specific risk judgments outside of the Pentagon, defense and military senior leaders should skillfully integrate the foundational terms suggested by this report into all DoD's communication with defense-focused communities of interest and practice.[4] Once established as a common point of departure, the foundational terms of reference pave the way for a more sophisticated articulation of risk outside of DoD.

Effective external communication starts with **diversity** and **dynamism** as seen through the medium of the principal risk portfolio. Post-primacy risk communication employing the portfolio and its four considerations of **importance, urgency, capability/capacity,** and **agility** provide risk consumers with an important perspective on the complexity and hazard associated with balancing competing military demands, identifying trade space that may allow leadership to buy-down or meaningfully address urgent requirements or see risk more clearly in order to accept or ride it out.

The six critical risk considerations captured under **persistent dialogue** described earlier in Section VI are also effective tools for communicating important risk considerations to key decision-makers outside of DoD. They are set up to specifically see an "if that, then this" relationship between specific defense and military actions or choices over the near-, mid-, and long-terms. They purposefully make side-by-side comparisons of red and blue relationships. Moreover, they do so specifically for both DoD and defense-interested senior leadership to understand the consequences of an increasingly diverse and dynamic challenge and response menu.

Finally, the concept of **adaptation** affords DoD senior leadership with a meaningful point of reference against which to focus and articulate the insights derived from examination of the portfolio (**diversity** and **dynamism**), as well as those emerging from DoD's persistent internal risk-focused **dialogue**. Communicating essential risk-informed **adaptations** to strategy, plans, programs, concepts, and capabilities in the most compelling way requires senior leadership to effectively place those proposed changes in the most appropriate context.

According to a member of the study's senior review group (SRG), that context is one of "competitive circumstances where there will be winners and losers."[5] In short, post-primacy will require persistent risk-informed dialogue within DoD that has as its purposes persistent risk-driven defense and military **adaptation**. To the extent DoD senior leadership allows the post-primacy narrative to take hold, focuses risk assessment on adaptation, and frames internal and external communication in the context of succeeding in a hyper-competitive environment, the likelier it is that any significant DoD course corrections will survive scrutiny. Again, drawing on important insights from the study's SRG, risk communication is "about the story."[6] The same SRG member concluded that DoD "need[s] to start explaining the story in a more compelling way."[7] Though jarring to many traditionalists, post-primacy and its prospective irreparable loss of strategic position are extremely compelling.

ENDNOTES – SECTION VII

1. See the September 5, 2014, consultation draft, Andy Bulgin, "Risk Communication in the 21st Century Extended Enterprise," in Institute of Risk Management, *Extended Enterprise: Managing Risk in Complex 21st Century Organizations, Institute of Risk Management*, London, UK: Institute of Risk Management, 2014, available from *https://www.theirm.org/knowledge-and-resources/thought-leadership/risks-in-the-extended-enterprise/extended-enterprise-documents.aspx*, accessed May 13, 2017.

2. James Thurber, quoted in *Ibid.*, p. 14.

3. This quoted insight came from a senior service representative during consultations at the Pentagon, Washington, DC, April 11, 2017.

4. The principal author of this report had experience in this regard when in the development of the 2005 *National Defense Strategy of the United States of America* (NDS), he and the strategy team began inserting new language and new definitions from the as yet unpublished strategy into reports and dialogues with the interagency and Congress.

5. This quoted reference was made by a senior review group (SRG) member during consultations at National Defense University, Washington, DC, March 30, 2017.

6. *Ibid.*

7. *Ibid.*

STUDY OUTCOMES

VIII. FINDINGS AND RECOMMENDATIONS

The biggest risk is not taking any risk. . . . In a world that's changing really quickly, the only strategy that is guaranteed to fail is not taking risk.[1]

Between July 2016 and April 2017, 9 months of intensive research and engagement with a wide variety of the Department of Defense (DoD) and defense-interested experts led the U.S. Army War College (USAWC) study team to the following four major findings and six associated actionable recommendations on the topic of post-primacy risk identification and assessment. The findings and recommendations are collected in like-types. Thus, multiple findings may be associated with a single recommendation or conversely a single finding may have multiple recommendations connected to it.

The insights here represent the best collective judgment and wisdom of the dozens of important voices engaged in the subjects of strategy development, strategic planning, and risk identification and assessment. The study team recommends that DoD carefully consider their integration into future strategy development and strategic planning processes. This is especially important now as DoD engages in development of a new *National Defense Strategy* (NDS).

This study identified four major findings for consideration by senior DoD leadership:

- *Contemporary defense strategy development and risk assessment will occur under post-primacy circumstances.*

- *Enterprise-level risk does not exist absent meaningful intentions, strategic objectives, or courses of action.*

- *Enterprise-level risk assessment should be an uncomplicated but not unsophisticated dialogue.*

- *Post-primacy strategic conditions will demand more federated approaches to risk assessment.*

FINDING 1

Contemporary defense strategy development and risk assessment will occur under post-primacy circumstances. In Section V, this study laid out five foundational characteristics of the post-primacy decision-making environment. They included hyperconnectivity, a fracturing post-Cold War status quo, the proliferation of counter-U.S. resistance, transformed great power competition, and the dissolution of political cohesion and identity worldwide. Post-primacy is not—as some might suggest—a defeatist perspective.[2] Instead, it is a passionate plea against complacency. It is the cold, calculating, and reasonable recognition of new levels of American vulnerability in an environment where the **capability** and **capacity** for strategic-level harm focused against core U.S. interests transcends boundaries, warfighting domains, and traditional defense conventions and biases.

Recognition that the remaining vestiges of a U.S.-friendly status quo are under "persistent assault" from a variety of purposeful and contextual forces will serve senior defense and military leadership well as they design strategy and assess risk less from the illusion of invincibility and more from the certainty of contested position and power.[3]

Post-primacy conditions require more sophistication in identifying and understanding the character of meaningful defense-relevant hazards; focusing, developing, and prudently adapting defense and military strategy; and finally, targeting and gaining meaningful insights from enterprise-level risk assessment. The manifold vectors of consequential, defense-relevant hazards are manifesting in ways that will increasingly cause senior defense and military leadership to work harder and smarter. Moreover, consequently, constructing effective strategy and identifying and assessing the nature and magnitude of corporate-level risks associated with it will be increasingly complex affairs.

FINDING 2

Enterprise-level risk does not exist absent meaningful intentions, strategic objectives, or courses of action. Many across DoD perceive risk identification and assessment to be excessively focused on the most tangible near-term threats—exemplified in the "4 plus 1" construct.[4] Furthermore, others would argue that there is no common or meaningful perspective on assessing corporate-level risk to the adopted defense strategy and its objectives. The study team suggests that these perspectives have significant merit. Moreover, to the extent that both are insights that are more or less true, the likelier it is that they create their own unique hidden risks.

What this report calls the operative threat-based approach to risk assessment is prone to miss significant defense-relevant hazards emerging from outside of DoD's current risk models. The defense enterprise may ultimately be ready for the most exquisitely armed 21st-century military threats but, at the same time, profoundly vulnerable to the very purposeful and contextual hazards that sit just outside prevailing convention and are more likely to emerge as important and urgent generators of surge demand. Indeed, one staff officer encountered through the study effort observed, "One of the most pernicious aspects of the current system of risk analysis across DoD is its tendency to link risks directly to a list of potential threats."[5]

This study makes six major recommendations for consideration by senior DoD leadership:

- *Adopt an objectives-based vice threat-based approach to enterprise-level risk assessment.*
- *Build a strategy-focused risk concept around four governing principles: diversity, dynamism, persistent dialogue, and adaptation.*
- *Pace DoD's risk assessment against a principal risk portfolio.*
- *Issue stand-alone, secretary-level risk guidance as a part of the strategy development process.*
- *Integrate interagency insights into DoD risk assessment and "lead-up" as trusted partners toward a common "whole of government" risk picture.*
- *Integrate core allies and partners into the risk assessment process.*

In the post-primacy environment, threat-based strategy development and risk assessment satisfy DoD's basest, most self-limiting corporate biases. Strategic planning, concepts, doctrine, acquisition, training, and education are all pegged to the same conventions and as such have the potential to unwittingly abet the compounding of corporate-level **strategic** and **military risk**. In short, DoD's long-standing traditional bias and convention likely help it immensely with problems it wants in the abstract while failing to adequately prepare it for the problems it has or will have in reality.

Risk identification and assessment, therefore, should be the product of calculated choices based on objectives embedded in a coherent strategic design. Paraphrasing one senior allied officer, you cannot assess risk unless you are actively taking it.[6] Thus, what might pass as risk in some quarters is simply an unrefined articulation of menace having little or no connection to strategic intentions, courses of action, or objectives.

This study suggests that purely threat-based approaches to either strategy or risk assessment can quickly devolve into conceptual dead ends that blind senior leadership, strategists, and planners to more compelling hazards equally deserving of their immediate attention. In the end, the best enterprise-level risk judgments will emerge from side-by-side comparisons of objectives, hazards, strategy, demands, and institutional priorities. In isolation, none of these could be expected to yield the comprehensive, high-impact risk-insights essential to post-primacy success.

Recommendation.

Adopt an objectives-based vice threat-based approach to enterprise-level risk assessment. This report argues for a strategy-focused risk identification and assessment **dialogue** that starts with broad understanding of DoD's core objectives, the environment within which those of objectives are secured, and the strategic approach associated with securing them. It links the enduring defense objectives to the most compelling 21st-century hazards. In the process, it leaves decision-makers with a clearer understanding of the environment's most important and urgent near-, mid-, and long-term defense and military demands. This unbroken connection between objectives, environment, strategy, and demands offers decision-makers a powerful tool with which to make reasonable risk-informed trades over time and at different levels of decision and action.

FINDING 3

Enterprise-level risk assessment should be an uncomplicated but not unsophisticated dialogue. In reality, risk judgments are negotiating positions in enterprise-level strategy development. They are not as some might suggest definitive or enduring statements of hazard.

The sage words of President Eisenhower are instructive here, "Plans are worthless, but planning is everything."[7] Paraphrasing Eisenhower and in the context of **strategic** and **military risk** identification and assessment, final risk judgments—high, medium, low, significant, etc.—may be far less useful for senior defense and military decision-makers than are the structured **dialogue** and its substantive debates employed to arrive at those judgments. Thus, DoD should commit to a high-level risk **dialogue** that focuses less on either process or final product and more on comprehensive understanding of the objective-hazard-demand relationship. A high-level risk dialogue that starts with strategic objectives and strategy and concludes with a broad consensus understanding of DoD's pacing demands and its inherent vulnerabilities will yield meaningful and actionable enterprise-level risk insights.

Risk identification and assessment should be uncomplicated but not unsophisticated. The insights derived from both should be the product of a simple parsimonious approach to identify and assess the impact on strategy and strategic objectives of the most salient hazards emerging from the post-primacy environment. They should focus on the most important defense-relevant issues impacting success of a chosen strategy while avoiding esoteric, obscure, or cryptic processes that only serve, according to one senior Army official, to "numb" both risk assessors and risk consumers.[8]

At the very moment that transformational strategic conditions demand equally transformational approaches to securing enduring defense objectives, complex corporate risk judgments that remain overly dependent on near-term or lagging indicators as primary data points will not provide senior defense and military leaders with the right perspectives for cross-cutting risk-based decisions.

If **adaptation** is in fact the point of all DoD's risk activity along the two critical axes (military/strategic and operational/future challenges) described in this report, the most important **adaptations** are those focused on the near-, mid-, and long-term interaction between U.S. strategy and the myriad purposeful and contextual adversaries and forces militating against it. A basic high-level **dialogue** that fully accounts for risk insights along these two axes provides the best start point from which DoD's senior leadership might proceed to craft a more diverse and dynamic approach to strategy development and risk assessment.

In this regard, this study finds that the best risk judgments should be products of two meaningful risk-focused ideas: First, an iterative and well-structured strategic **dialogue** focused early on a comprehensive understanding of strategy and strategic objectives in the context of the decision-making environment. Second, in addition to strategic **dialogue**, meaningful recommendations for persistent **adaptation** of strategy, plans, concepts, capabilities, and material **capacity** to effectively confront key asymmetries between what is truly important and urgent, and what is actually being done about it.

Recommendation.

Build a strategy-focused risk concept around four core principles: diversity, dynamism, persistent dialogue, and adaptation. Section V described the four principles this study suggests underpin a new more fulsome enterprise-level risk **dialogue** for DoD. They are the living foundation of an uncomplicated but not unsophisticated approach to post-primacy risk identification and assessment. First, the study argues that DoD must account for a more diverse set of strategic-level hazards and associated important and urgent defense demands. Proceeding from the recognition that DoD has a perfect record in its failure to predict its highest-priority contingency requirements, this study argues that an effective hedge against that perfect record is broadening the aperture DoD employs for risk identification and assessment.[9]

Second, the study team and the universe of DoD and defense-interested stakeholders the team engaged with in the course of the work concluded that current risk conventions lacked the requisite **dynamism** essential to keeping up with rapidly changing post-primacy strategic conditions. Thus, any new concept or approach to corporate-level risk must account for inherent **dynamism** in the nature, character, and sequencing of compelling defense-relevant hazards, as well as in unavoidable (unforeseen, or underprepared for) changes that occur in DoD's **capability** and **capacity** to act with purpose against them. In short, there is nothing static about DoD's strategic approach to the world, the hazards it may encounter pursuing that approach, or the responses DoD will marshal to contend with those hazards. Thus, risk identification and assessment must benefit from a built-in commitment to look and account for dynamic endogenous and exogenous change.

The third principle—**persistent dialogue**—implores the defense enterprise to find a meaningful path by which it thoroughly explores risk along two important and inseparable axes (military/strategic and operational/future challenges). Persistence in this endeavor is required in response to the velocity and high-consequence of ceaseless change in the hazards emerging from the environment. Suffice it to say that the combination of **diversity** in defense-relevant hazards and responses, as well as the **dynamism** exhibited of late by both, necessitate a disciplined and diligent approach to monitoring change and assessing its impact on the 10-year defense outlook. Combined, the principles of **diversity**, **dynamism**, and **persistent dialogue** buffer the enterprise against disruptive surprise and shock.

Finally, the study team argues that in addition to a direct connection back to objectives and strategic courses of action, all risk assessments should have a point. In the end, the focus or purpose of risk assessment should be change. Sometimes that change is simply some broader and more meaningful understanding of the challenges at hand. However, more often, this study argues that all enterprise-level risk identification and assessment should focus squarely on helping senior defense and military leaders to adapt their institutions to high-volume, high-impact post-primacy change. With **adaptation** at its core, risk assessment becomes an exercise in agile problem solving and not one of endless problem identification.

Recommendation.

Pace DoD's risk assessment against a principal risk portfolio. This study has described in great detail what it believes is the start point for meaningful post-primacy risk assessment. The principal risk portfolio is the strategy and objectives-based expression of important and urgent military demand against which DoD should persistently assess and apportion risk over the near-, mid-, and long-terms.

This report offered both illustrative enduring defense objectives and illustrative 10-year surge demands as a way of demonstrating the portfolio's utility in the context of the four driving post-primacy risk principles—**diversity**, **dynamism**, **persistent dialogue**, and **adaptation**. In the end, the portfolio is intended to be a living reservoir where defense and military senior leadership collect DoD's most important and urgent surge demands for constant assessment against evolutionary and revolutionary change in strategic conditions. The portfolio is not the sum total of DoD's mission set. It is a reflection of anticipated surge demand and the abiding responsibility of defense senior leadership to meet those demands first according to some prioritization.

The portfolio itself has four governing concepts—**importance**, **urgency**, **capability/capacity**, and **agility**. Broad understanding of the relationship between and among all four provide senior defense and military leadership with opportunities for a continuous discourse on where DoD might be able to accept, mitigate, avoid, or transfer identified risk.

Because the portfolio—like the larger strategy and risk debate—is a living construct, it must change, as a routine part of the **persistent dialogue** discussed earlier. New demands will supplant existing requirements. Moreover, existing demands will rise and fall in **importance** and **urgency** as the environment changes and extant asymmetries between **importance**, **urgency**, **capability/capacity**, and **agility** change or adapt to internal or external inputs. What the portfolio provides senior leaders is a centerpiece for a meaningful discussion of risk allocation under circumstances of persistent external adjustment and internal **adaptation**.

Recommendation.

Issue stand-alone, secretary-level risk guidance as a part of the strategy development process. Late in the study effort, the team encountered a thoughtful discussion on risk "ownership."[10] It led the team to ask and answer a final important question: Who owns corporate risk within DoD? While recognizing the central role of the Chairman of the Joint Chiefs of Staff (CJCS) as the secretary's principal military advisor, the team recognized that there could only be one answer to that question—the Secretary of Defense.[11] Thus, in consultation with key DoD and defense-interested stakeholders, the study team determined that DoD and its constituent service components and defense agencies would benefit from classified, secretary-level guidance on risk. That guidance should outline the secretary's corporate priorities and trades related to risk—expressed in the common risk currency discussed throughout this report.

The secretary's risk guidance should reflect a thoughtful appreciation of the two primary axes of risk identified throughout the study (military/strategic and operational/future challenges). Naturally, in practice, the team suggests that this guidance is developed in close collaboration with the CJCS. The study team concluded that the guidance must demonstrate a clear appreciation for: 1) a measurable set of enduring defense objectives; 2) an extant strategy or strategic terms of reference (incorporating those objectives); and finally, 3) the four governing principles of risk assessment. Again, the latter includes: **diversity** in the hazards and demands considered; recognition of the environment's **dynamism** and propensity for change; acknowledgment of the insights gathered throughout a process of **persistent dialogue;** and finally, a commitment to relentless conditions-based **adaptation**.

A classified, secretary-level statement of risk-related priorities and trades—at the beginning of a presidential term and updated every other year—will put DoD on a common, less internally-competitive strategic foundation. It will communicate to DoD and those constituencies most interested in DoD's strategic choices where and under what circumstances the secretary has determined that DoD will accept, mitigate, transfer, and avoid risk.

There was concern among some consulted that this guidance would encroach on the Title 10 responsibilities of service chiefs, extant processes associated with the Chairman's Risk Assessment (CRA), and long-standing tradition or conventions about DoD's internal division of labor.[12] Mindful of these concerns, the study team suggests that this guidance complement vice compete with extant risk mechanisms. For example, in light of the near-term focus of the CRA, the study team suggests that the secretary's guidance adopt a longer time horizon that informs near-term risk choices but also provides clear, detailed guidance on the dead space starting on the high margin of near-term or operational risk and running through longer-term **future challenges risk** (and, at both the strategic and military levels of analysis). Likewise, the study team would argue that another important contribution of this guidance would be articulating clear prioritization between strategic choices that are in obvious competition with one another, as well as recommendations on how priorities might change over time with changes in strategic conditions.

FINDING 4

Post-primacy strategic conditions will demand more federated approaches to risk assessment. Among the more predictable aspects of study efforts like this are two common observations by participants: 1) "This is not just a DoD problem alone. Do not forget the interagency," and 2) "This is not an American problem alone. Do not forget the allies and partners." The study is mindful of both critiques and recognizes that there could and should be more federated approaches first to strategy development and strategic planning and then to risk identification and assessment.

Employing the principal risk portfolio and its four criteria within the context of a new concept emphasizing **diversity**, **dynamism**, **persistent dialogue**, and **adaptation**, corporate-level defense risk assessment would benefit from the insights of DoD's interagency and allied partners. For starters, the corporate interests and biases of non-DoD partners will invariably differ from those of senior defense and military leadership. As a consequence, their participation in both strategy development, strategic planning, and risk assessment will no doubt contribute new and important perspectives to the defense strategy and risk **dialogue**. From a more utilitarian standpoint, the same partners might recognize, through the **dialogue**, that they are essential contributors to **capability/capacity** shortfalls or they are best postured to lead or make significant contributions to increase **agility**. In short, and in a world of exploding demand, DoD's civilian and military partners may be critical levers for risk mitigation, avoidance, or transfer.

In the end, more federated approaches to risk identification and assessment are essential to post-primacy success. As noted at multiple points in this report, consequential hazards are multiplying, metastasizing, and morphing to such an extent that the U.S. military can no longer hope to favorably influence security outcomes everywhere and every time it prefers. However, it substantially increases its odds of doing so in the face of the most important and urgent hazards by integrating the insights and contributions of a broad and diverse universe of civilian-military partners. Success in this regard will require immediate changes (i.e., additions) in who DoD allows into its strategy and risk assessment processes.

Recommendation.

Integrate interagency insights into DoD risk assessment and then "lead-up" as trusted partners toward a common "whole of government" risk picture. Given finding 4, the study identified two important innovations with respect to risk identification and assessment as it relates to the interagency. First, DoD should integrate key interagency partners in every level of its ongoing strategy and risk **dialogues**. This includes but is not limited to the civilian intelligence community, as well as the Departments of State, Homeland Security, and Justice. Their participation is a sign of good faith, an informed source of alternative perspectives, and, in the end, is instructive for all involved on where and how non-DoD contributions will make a difference in securing **enduring defense objectives** and reducing excessive risk.

The second innovation mirrors one of last year's gray zone recommendations. The gray zone study team suggested that DoD's culture of planning was best postured to help senior national security leaders see gray zone challenges clearly and understand the broad whole of government levers essential to combating them effectively. That same culture of planning and its rhetorical commitment (at a minimum) to risk-based decision-making suggests that DoD again lead-up in the area of whole of government strategy development and, more specifically, risk assessment. Through the initial act of good faith associated with bringing interagency partners into its own internal risk identification and assessment process, DoD might advance the concept of whole of government risk-based decision-making across the national security community.

There may be significant trust issues for senior DoD leaders to overcome if DoD is to successfully lead-up on the subject of risk. Nonetheless, it was clear to the study team and those that it engaged with over the course of the research effort that top-down articulations of actionable strategy and risk guidance would improve overall U.S. Government performance. This improved performance would materially benefit DoD's defense of **enduring defense objectives**.

Recommendation.

Integrate core allies and partners into the risk assessment process. Post-primacy is no time to act alone. Despite the common refrain that the United States will act with others when it can and unilaterally when it must, allies and partners are increasingly an indispensable U.S. strategic hedge. The United States has two basic types of defense alliances and partnerships.

First, there is the regional variety. According to either treaty or convention, regional allies and partners help the United States maintain favorable security conditions within regions whose stability is essential to U.S. security. Japan and the Republic of Korea in the Pacific, and Egypt, Saudi Arabia, Jordan, and Israel in the Middle East come to mind in this regard. Obviously, the North Atlantic Treaty Organization (NATO) Alliance is a clear example of a regionally-based entente as well. The U.S. position in those regions by and large relies on stable bi- or multi-lateral relations, as well as routine and in extremis military cooperation.

The second global variety of ally and partner helps the United States maintain stability in their region as well, while also reliably participating in the more general policing of the international status quo that they all prefer and benefit from. Much has been said already on the vulnerability of that preferred status quo. This category includes many NATO nations. However, the United Kingdom, Australia, Canada, and France are particularly active U.S. global partners.

Many of these global partnerships are becoming much more conditional. This may be a function of increased nationalism and its attendant focus on self-interest first. However, it is also likely a function of the proliferation, diversification, and atomization of effective counter-U.S. and counter-Western resistance as well. Hazards are manifesting in different ways at different times to individual states. Consequently, it is more challenging to generate a common perspective on objectives, vulnerabilities, strategies, demands, and priorities.

In spite of this profound lack of clarity in strategic conditions among and between allies and partners, the study team suggests that every effort should be made to harmonize their collective perspectives on strategy and risk within regions and with regionally-based allies, which requires cooperative alliance (or partnership) management.[13] Post-primacy will require some humility on the part of the United States in this regard, because, increasingly, self-interest trumps collective interest.

The United States will need to approach global allies with a similar tack. In some respects, however, alliance (or partnership) cohesion may be a tougher sell. "Away games" are increasingly more difficult to sell to war weary populations. Combined with the prospect of hyperconnectivity bringing more problems home, the United States should focus its risk harmonization first on those allies and partners with whom it is likeliest to rely on for worldwide coalition action. Often, the regional allies and partners see the local threats more clearly.

In the end, regardless of whether or not allies and partners are regional or global in their orientation, the United States will rely on their political will and material strength to offset risks associated with increasing hazard. As was suggested earlier, the United States will need to work harder and smarter to retain a favorable global position and the freedom of action necessary to maintain it. This will not happen without the active cooperation of the United States' network of alliances and partnerships.

One clear path to their active cooperation includes their being fully incorporated to the extent possible in DoD's persistent risk **dialogue**. Failure in this regard invites the fatal traps of unrealistic expectations, overreach, miscalculation, and ultimately, unexpected failure or cost on the part of the United States. Dealing allies and partners into corporate risk identification and assessment, on the other hand, fosters a common understanding of hazard and demand that may result in more equitable or more effective burden sharing.

ENDNOTES – SECTION VIII

1. Mark Zuckerberg quoted in Steve Tobak, "Facebook's Mark Zuckerberg—Insights For Entrepreneurs," *Moneywatch*, CBS, October 31, 2011, available from *www.cbsnews.com/news/facebooks-mark-zuckerberg-insights-for-entrepreneurs/*, accessed May 8, 2017.

2. The concept of "post-primacy" was widely acknowledged by the vast majority of those the study team engaged with during the course of the study. It was, however, a source of significant discomfort for some senior leaders engaged in the course of the study. Because of the wide majority acknowledgement of the term as appropriate to current strategic conditions, the U.S. Army War College (USAWC) study opted to retain it as an organizing principle for the report.

3. Nathan Freier, proj. dir., Charles R. Burnett, William J. Cain, Jr., Christopher D. Compton, Sean M. Hankard, Robert S. Hume, Gary R. Kramlich II, J. Matthew Lissner, Tobin A. Magsig, Daniel E. Mouton, Michael S. Muztafago, James M. Schultze, John F. Troxell, and Dennis G. Wille, cont. auths., *Outplayed: Regaining Strategic Initiative in the Gray Zone*, Carlisle, PA: Strategic Studies Institute, U.S. Army War College, 2016, p. 19, available from *ssi.armywarcollege.edu/pubs/display.cfm?pubID=1325,* accessed May 3, 2017.

4. See another recent reference to the Pentagon's "4 plus 1" threat construct in Fred Dews, "Joint Chiefs Chairman Dunford on the '4 + 1 framework' and meeting transnational threats," February 24, 2017, available from *https://www.brookings.edu/blog/brookings-now/2017/02/24/joint-chiefs-chairman-dunford-transnational-threats/*, accessed April 25, 2017.

5. U.S. Special Operations Command (USSOCOM), "Risk Concept Paper," unpublished staff paper provided to the study team on a visit to USSOCOM headquarters at MacDill Air Force Base, FL, January 17, 2017, p. 4.

6. This insight emerged from a roundtable discussion with two allied officers in Honolulu, Hawaii, March 6, 2017.

7. Dwight D. Eisenhower, "Remarks at the National Defense Executive Reserve Conference," November 14, 1957, available from *www.presidency.ucsb.edu/ws/?pid=10951*, accessed April 21, 2017.

8. This quoted insight was derived from consultation with senior Army officials in the Pentagon, Washington, DC, April 11, 2017.

9. See Micah Zenko, "100% Right 0% of the Time: Why the U.S. military can't predict the next war," *Foreign Policy*, October 16, 2012, available from *foreignpolicy.com/2012/10/16/100-right-0-of-the-time/*, accessed April 25, 2017.

10. This insight emerged from a private roundtable discussion with a senior U.S. military officer at the USAWC, Carlisle, PA, April 12, 2017.

11. Though the Chairman's role in risk assessment is codified in U.S. Code, the team recognized that the Secretary's position in the chain of command indicated "ownership" over enterprise level risk over the near-, mid-, and long-term along the military to strategic continuum.

12. This insight was particularly evident in consultation with a senior service official in the Pentagon, Washington, DC, April 11, 2017.

13. This insight was central to consultations with key staff of a sub-unified command in the U.S. Pacific Command (USPACOM) Area of Responsibility (AoR), March 8, 2017.

IX. CONCLUSION—OWNERSHIP, CULTURE, AND ADAPTATION

Every word in the title of this study is purposeful—*At Our Own Peril: DoD Risk Assessment in a Post-Primacy World*. The title conveys an urgency the study team detected among defense and defense-interested communities about the need to change or update the Department of Defense's (DoD) corporate perspective on both strategy development and risk assessment. Indeed, the study team detected a general unease or discomfort with current conventions on both counts. This is not an indictment of existing processes like the Chairman's Risk Assessment (CRA). It is rather an acknowledgement that current convention is insufficient given contemporary hazards and demands.

While defense and military professionals work hard to secure U.S. interests with the tools at their disposal, this study discovered that many among them and those that inform them believe current strategy and risk conventions are simply ill-suited or inadequate for contemporary strategic circumstances. Current risk concepts in particular are excessively focused on near-term considerations or straight-line extrapolations of the near-term forward. These perspectives harbor the potential to mortgage both future success and near-term off-script performance. In short, the environment is increasingly defined by discontinuity, persistent revolutionary change, and U.S. vulnerability while DoD's strategy, planning, and risk assessment models favor predictability, evolution, and unchallenged U.S. advantage.

There is a clear and unambiguous recognition of this in virtually every quarter of the defense establishment this effort engaged with over the previous year. There is universal recognition as well that the United States and its defense establishment no longer exercise the degree of unchallenged strategic dominance enjoyed from the end of the Cold War through the immediate post-9/11 period. Those engaged in the work of strategy and risk also recognize that they are navigating an era of hyper-competition where standard responses, default solutions, and raw aggregate potential are insufficient remedies for the myriad strategic hazards they now confront.

In response, they are also aware that regaining and maintaining an unassailable position of American military advantage will require new perspectives and approaches to strategy and risk. In a word, defense and military professionals understand that they must adjust to profound environmental change and do so persistently based on deliberate strategic choices that are informed by new insights on risk. The perceived urgency springs from a collective sense among many senior and working-level defense and military professionals that the margins for error are increasingly tightening.

This study endeavored to provide senior DoD leadership with advice in this regard. Over the course of 9 months of intensive research and engagement with defense-focused communities of interest and practice, the study arrived at a finite number of actionable findings and recommendations for senior defense leadership. However, as important as these findings and recommendations are, the study team discovered three additional foundational insights that are an apt way of closing the report. These insights involve—**risk ownership, risk as culture,** and **risk as an instrument for adaptation**.

First, clear unambiguous corporate-level **risk ownership** will help DoD recalibrate to a more complex strategic environment. In order for strategic guidance and risk judgments to permeate DoD and inform all senior leader decision-making;

responsibility, authority, and ownership of risk should be unambiguously aligned.[1] The team would suggest that enterprise-level risk assessment is a shared responsibility between the Secretary of Defense and the Chairman of the Joint Chiefs of Staff (CJCS). Recall, for example, the study's description of top-down and bottom-up risk assessments along the military-to-strategic continuum and across the time horizon of operational-to-future challenges. Where corporate ownership clearly leans toward Secretaries of Defense is in the combination of their responsibility for assessment and their authority to do something about the findings of assessments.

Through persistent, collaborative risk assessment and consultation with the CJCS, the Secretary can and should exercise risk leadership for DoD. While the study suggests that consultation will come in the form of specific risk guidance during strategy development, it should also permeate all decisions and processes over which the secretary has authority. Employment of the common risk currency described in this report will help in this regard.

An enterprise-wide approach is appropriate for setting objectives across the organization, instilling an enterprise-wide culture, and ensuring that key activities and risks are monitored regularly. Senior management must be in [enterprise risk management], since they are the ones who decide the level and types of risk the organization is comfortable with accepting and what controls and risk mitigants will be employed to ensure that risk exposures stay within the agreed-upon levels.[2]

None of this is meant to suggest that others in DoD senior leadership—in particular, the Joint Chiefs of Staff (JCS) and the combatant commands—do not have their own risk responsibilities and authorities. However, as Secretaries of Defense are the senior-most DoD officers in the military chain of command, they must then ultimately also own enterprise-level risk and speak with authority on it.

A second foundational insight is the idea of **risk as a culture**. Risk identification and assessment cannot simply be a process, a product, or a static judgment on hazard or danger. It needs to be a persistent component of DoD's corporate culture. Consistent with the first insight, risk identification and assessment needs to permeate DoD's strategic dialogue and remain central to all the consequential DoD decision-making.

This report suggests that risk identification and assessment need to involve the constant side-by-side comparison of objectives, the environment and hazards, strategies, demands, and institutional priorities. If it remains a once a year or once every 2 years staff exercise, and if it fails to account for the totality of the two key axes of assessment (military/strategic and operational/future challenges), contemporary events will outpace and overwhelm DoD. Moreover, consequently, failure and/or unacceptable cost will follow to the great detriment of its overall performance.

Finally, on the subject of **risk as an instrument of adaptation**, the findings are unequivocal. Any and all corporate-level risk identification and assessment within DoD must have as its expressed purpose adaptation to ever-changing strategic circumstances. The study team has outlined a risk concept with four governing principles: **diversity**, **dynamism**, **persistent dialogue**, and finally, **adaptation**. The last is the most important among them.

Why **diversity, dynamism**, and **persistent dialogue**? The answer is, in a word, **adaptation**. Because DoD is required to demonstrate a persistent commitment to defend at-risk interests, objectives, and partners now and over time and because the environment is subject to constant consequential change, meeting basic 21st-century defense obligations requires constant, unrelenting, risk-informed adaptation.

In the final analysis, this report argues for a corporate risk model founded on persistent senior leader dialogue and fine-tuned to monitor and adapt to constant change in strategic conditions. Maintenance of U.S. defense and military advantage is at stake. DoD's future risk concept should proceed from that weighty and potentially grave point of departure. Short of that, DoD exposes current and future performance to significant unrecognized or under-recognized hazard.

ENDNOTES – SECTION IX

1. The concept of aligning risk authority, responsibility, and ownership emerged from insights derived both from a group interaction with a senior theater commander in April 2017 in Carlisle, PA, as well as from a one-on-one discussion with a former senior civilian DoD official also in April 2017, but in Washington, DC.

2. Governor Susan Schmidt Bies, "A Bank Supervisor's Perspective on Enterprise Risk Management," Speech at the Enterprise Risk Management Roundtable, North Carolina State University, Raleigh, North Carolina, April 28, 2006, available from *https://www.federalreserve.gov/newsevents/speech/Bies20060428a.htm*, accessed May 3, 2017.

APPENDICES

APPENDIX I - BUILDING THE PRINCIPAL RISK PORTFOLIO: ILLUSTRATIVE HAZARDS AND DEMANDS

Early in the study, the U.S. Army War College (USAWC) study team surveyed defense-interested communities of interest and practice in order to gauge the range of the most important potential 10-year surge demands. The team contributed their own responses as well. Figure AI-1 represents an aggregation and synthesis of the replies to the question: "What do you perceive to be the Department of Defense's (DoD's) top 5 potential **surge** military demands between 2017-2027?"

The illustrative hazards in the left hand column are not intended to be predictive. Instead, they are descriptive of the kinds of hazards that could generate the surge military demands outlined in the right column. The illustrative hazards listed here are a reflection of the kinds of potential hazards and demands anticipated by defense and military professionals over the next decade. Use of the hazards in this report was strictly limited to identification of generic 10-year surge demands. Once identified, the demands were aggregated into the illustrative principal risk portfolio described in this report.

Building the Principal Risk Portfolio: Illustrative Hazards and Demand Types

Raw Illustrative Hazards	Prospective Surge Demands
• Perceived Loss of Nuclear/Tech Advantage • Future Gulf Nuclear Stand-Off • People's Republic of China/Russian Counter-Space Campaign	Strategic Deterrence and Defense
• Russian Gray/Black Campaign Against the North Atlantic Treaty Organization (NATO) Member States • People's Republic of China Gray/Black Campaign to Seize Taiwan • Russia/People's Republic of China/Iran Gray/Black Campaign Against U.S. Global Position • Regional Iranian Hybrid War	Gray Zone/Counter-Gray Zone
• Russian Baltic Counter-Access Campaign • People's Republic of China Counter-Access Campaign	Access/Anti-Access
• People's Republic of China Annexation of the South China Seas and Isolation of Japan/the East China Sea • Democratic People's Republic of Korea Conventional/Nuclear Aggression Against the Republic of Korea/Japan	Major Combat
• Russia Civil War/Loss of Control Over Nuclear Arsenal • Pakistan Civil Conflict/Loss of Control Over Nuclear Arsenal • Contagious Pan-Regional Military Engagement Civil Conflict • Widespread Mexican Civil Conflict/Migration Crisis • Democratic People's Republic of Korea Collapse, Civil Conflict, Loss of Control over Weapons of Mass Destruction • Turkish Civil Conflict	Distributed Security
• Competitor Strategic Manipulation of Perceptions to Achieve Favorable Strategic Outcomes • Effective Cyber/Info Campaign Against U.S. Global Position	Influence/Counter Influence
• Transnational Sunni-Shia Sectarian Civil Conflict • Globally Distributed Terrorist Campaign	Counter-Network
• Domestic Public Health Emergency • Large-Scale Domestic Disaster	Humanitarian Assistance and Consequence Management

} Draft Principal Risk Portfolio

The principal risk portfolio is the aggregation of pacing defense demands used to assess risk.

Figure AI-1. Illustrative Hazards and Demands.

APPENDIX II - EXPERT WORKING GROUP (EWG) PARTICIPANTS

Dr. Don Allen, Ph.D., Air Staff.

Lieutenant Colonel (LTC) Steven Barry, U.S. Army, Joint Staff, J-5.

Colonel (COL) Susan Bryant, U.S. Army, Institute for National Strategic Studies, National Defense University.

Colonel (Col) Mark Cancian, U.S. Marine Corps, Retired, Center for Strategic and International Studies (CSIS).

Mr. J.D. Canty, U.S. Marine Corps Combat Development Command.

Dr. Alex Crowther, Ph.D., Institute for National Strategic Studies, National Defense University.

Lieutenant Colonel (Lt Col) Jonathan Dagle, U.S. Air Force, Retired, JD Solutions, Limited Liability Company (LLC).

Ms. Melissa Dalton, CSIS.

Dr. Andrew Erdmann, Ph.D., McKinsey and Company.

Mr. Robert Haddick, Billy Mitchell Institute.

Colonel (COL) Jeffery Hannon, U.S. Army, Office of the Secretary of Defense (OSD).

Captain (CAPT) Robert Hein, U.S. Navy, Navy Staff.

Dr. Andrew Hill, Ph.D., U.S. Army War College (USAWC).

Dr. Frank Hoffman, Ph.D., Institute for National Strategic Studies, National Defense University.

Lepi Jha, McKinsey and Company.

Mr. Burgess Laird, RAND Corporation.

Mr. Phil Lohaus, American Enterprise Institute.

Colonel (COL) Dan MacGuire, U.S. Army, Retired, Consultant.

Ms. Laura McAleer, United States Senate.

Major (MAJ) Gabriel Morris, U.S. Army, Army Staff.

Mr. Tim Muchmore, U.S. Army Staff.

Lieutenant Commander (LCDR) Elizabeth Nelson, U.S. Navy, Joint Staff, J-5.

Colonel (Col) Craig Price, U.S. Marine Corps, Marine Corps War College.

Mr. Jay Rouse, Joint Staff, J-5.

Mr. Russell Rumbaugh, OSD.

Ms. Loren Schulman, Center for a New American Security.

Dr. Tammy Schultz, Ph.D., Marine Corps War College.

Lieutenant Colonel (LtCol) Mark Thieme, Headquarters, Marine Corps.

Lieutenant Colonel (LTC) James Turner, U.S. Army, Joint Staff, J-5.

Mr. Phil Walter, OSD.

APPENDIX III - ABOUT THE CONTRIBUTORS

PRINCIPAL AUTHOR AND PROJECT DIRECTOR

NATHAN P. FREIER is an Associate Professor of National Security Studies with the Strategic Studies Institute (SSI). He came to SSI in August 2013 after 5 years with the Center for Strategic and International Studies (CSIS) where he was a senior fellow in the International Security Program. Mr. Freier joined CSIS in April 2008 after completing a 20-year career in the U.S. Army. His last military assignment was as Director of National Security Affairs at SSI. From August 2008 to July 2012, Mr. Freier also served as a visiting research professor in strategy, policy, and risk assessment at the U.S. Army War College's Peacekeeping and Stability Operations Institute (PKSOI) under the provisions of the Intergovernmental Personnel Act. Mr. Freier is a veteran of numerous strategy development and strategic planning efforts at Headquarters, Department of the Army; the Office of the Secretary of Defense; and two senior-level military staffs in Iraq. Mr. Freier is widely published on a range of national security issues and continues to provide expert advice to the national security and defense communities. His areas of expertise are defense and military strategy and policy development and strategic net and risk assessment. He holds master's degrees in both international relations and politics and is a graduate of the U.S. Army's Command and General Staff College.

CONTRIBUTING AUTHORS

CHRISTOPHER M. BADO, Colonel (COL), U.S. Army, Retired, is a former Army strategist and previously served as the Chair of the Department of Military Planning, and Operations at the U.S. Army War College (USAWC) where he also held the John Shalikashvili Chair of Joint Military Studies. He has a deep background in strategic and operational planning with assignments at U.S. European Command, U.S. Africa Command, the Army Staff, and United States Forces—Iraq. He served on the faculty at the U.S. Military Academy at West Point and as the Army Strategic Fellow at the University of Maryland in the Center for International and Strategic Studies at Maryland (CISSM). His areas of expertise are military and defense strategy, strategic and operational art, campaign planning, and special operations and irregular warfare. He holds a bachelor of science in mathematics and economics from the University of California Santa Barbara and master's degrees in national security affairs and strategic studies from the Naval Postgraduate School and the Air War College respectively.

CHRISTOPHER J. BOLAN is the Professor of Middle East Security Studies with SSI. Dr. Bolan recently arrived at SSI after 11 years of teaching graduate courses on U.S. national security, international relations, strategy formulation, and the Middle East at the USAWC. He retired from the U.S. Army as a colonel after serving 30 years with tours in Egypt, Tunisia, Jordan, the Pentagon, and the White House. From 1996-2002, he served as a Middle East foreign policy advisor to both Vice Presidents Gore and Cheney. He has a master of arts degree in Arab studies and a Ph.D. in international relations from Georgetown University. He tweets on national security issues @DrChrisBolan.

ROBERT S. HUME, Colonel (COL), U.S. Army, Retired, is an assistant professor of operational art and theater planning at the USAWC. He began serving as a civilian professor of practice in 2014, following a 29-year career as an active Army officer (aviator, operations research systems analyst, and Army strategist) and culminating as a course director and faculty instructor in the USAWC Department of Distance Education. Professor Hume's primary duties include teaching resident students in the Theater Strategy and Campaigning core course, as well as teaching elective courses and advising students in completion of strategy research projects. Professor Hume's areas of expertise are defense strategy, campaign planning and assessment, strategic leadership, and defense management. He has a bachelor of science in engineering from the U.S. Military Academy at West Point, and holds master's degrees in both operations research and systems analysis from the Naval Postgraduate School and strategic studies from the USAWC.

J. MATTHEW LISSNER, Colonel (COL), has served in all three components of the Army (Active, National Guard, and Army Reserve) for over 28 years. Currently, he serves as the Senior Army Reserve Research Advisor, SSI, USAWC, at Carlisle Barracks, PA. He has held a wide variety of infantry assignments through battalion level with the 7th Infantry Division (Light), 11th Armored Cavalry Regiment Opposing Force (OPFOR), and the 39th Separate Infantry Brigade (Enhanced), and has held staff positions at the 77th Regional Readiness Command, Training and Doctrine Command (TRADOC), Third U.S. Army, U.S. Joint Forces Command, I Corps, and the 99th Regional Support Command. His combat deployments include Operation JUST CAUSE (Panama), Operation IRAQI FREEDOM/Operation ENDURING FREEDOM (Kuwait), and Operation IRAQI FREEDOM (Iraq).

CONTRIBUTING RESEARCHERS

HEATHER BELLUSCI, Lieutenant Colonel (LTC), is a 1996 graduate of Gonzaga University with a bachelor's degree in computer science. Additionally, she earned a master's degree in business administration with an emphasis in information technology from Webster University. LTC Bellusci served as Blackhawk helicopter pilot and maintenance commander for the first half of her career. She has deployed in support of Stabilization Forces in Bosnia-Herzegovina and Operation IRAQI FREEDOM. LTC Bellusci became a member of the Army Acquisition Corps in 2005. She has experience in program management and information technology within the Defense Information Systems Agency, Special Operations Command, and the Intelligence Community.

JOHN R. BEURER, Lieutenant Colonel (Lt Col) Beurer is a 1998 graduate of the United States Air Force Academy and received a master's degree from Bellevue University. He is a command pilot with over 19 years on active duty, holding a variety of command and staff positions. Lt Col Beurer deployed as an Air Advisor to the Afghan Air Corps and as the Combined Air Power Transition Force's Rotary Wing Program Manager in support of Operation ENDURING FREEDOM.

RALPH BORJA, Colonel (COL), is a 1994 graduate of the University of Guam and received a master's degree from the Naval Postgraduate School. He entered the Army as a field artillery officer and served in that capacity for 8 years. He is currently an acquisition officer and has held a variety of positions in contracting and program office organizations. COL Borja's deployments include Operation DESERT SPRING (Kuwait) and Operation ENDURING FREEDOM (Afghanistan).

STEVEN BUELT is a civilian program manager with the Defense Intelligence Agency (DIA). Mr. Buelt holds a bachelor's degree from Excelsior College and has over 33 years of national defense experience that includes 21 years active duty in the U.S. Army, 5 years in commercial industry in support of Department of Defense (DoD) programs, and 7 years in U.S. Government service. Mr. Buelt most recently served as the Deputy Chief of the Operations Training Department in DIA's Academy for Defense Intelligence, managing joint training programs for DoD. Mr. Buelt's military career includes multiple assignments in the XVIII Airborne Corps, U.S. Army Intelligence and Security Command, and the U.S. Army Special Operations Command (USASOC). Mr. Buelt's overseas assignments include Germany, Italy, and Korea, with deployments to Bosnia and Haiti.

MICHAEL LECHLITNER is an intelligence officer of the Central Intelligence Agency (CIA) with a long-term assignment to the National Geospatial-Intelligence Agency (NGA). His last position was as the Senior NGA Representative to the National Intelligence Council. Prior assignments have included Senior Government Site Lead/Processing, Exploitation and Dissemination Team Lead for three Intelligence, Surveillance and Reconnaissance (ISR) aircraft at Camp Bastion/Leatherneck, Afghanistan, and the NGA Representative to the Joint Improvised Explosive Device Defeat Organization (JIEDDO) under DoD. He has also served as Chief of Staff (acting) for the Analysis Directorate of NGA; as a division chief leading the integration effort of NGA analysts into National Security Agency Centers in Georgia, Texas, Colorado, and Hawaii; and as the Executive Officer of the Office of Eurasia-Africa at NGA. He deployed immediately after 9/11 as part of a National Intelligence Support Team working with 5th Special Forces Group in northern Afghanistan. Additionally, he was a member of the Conventional Armed Forces (CFE) Treaty delegation in Vienna, Austria, and a CFE and Intermediate-Range Nuclear Forces (INF) treaty inspector. He holds a bachelor's degree in political science with an emphasis on Russian and East European Studies from the University of Michigan and also served in the U.S. Army (enlisted).

ROBERT D. MONTZ, Lieutenant Colonel (LTC), is a 1997 graduate of the University of Pittsburgh with a bachelor of science in occupational therapy. He received a master's degree from University of Florida in health science and a doctorate degree from Rocky Mountain University of Health Professions. His last position was as the Executive Officer for the Command Surgeon, U.S. Army Forces Command. LTC Montz has deployed on six occasions to support Operation ENDURING FREEDOM and Operation IRAQI FREEDOM in various capacities. His area of expertise is in the rehabilitation, human performance, and resilience arenas. He has worked in a variety of environments to include U.S. Special Operations Command (USSOCOM), Army Medical Command, and U.S. Army Forces Command.

ROBERT PHILLIPS, Colonel (COL), has a bachelor's degree from West Virginia University, a master's degree in business administration, and master of arts degree in public administration from Syracuse University. He has served in the U.S. Army for over 22 years as an infantry and finance officer, deploying twice to Iraq in support of Operation IRAQI FREEDOM and Operation NEW DAWN. COL Phillips recently served as the comptroller for the 82nd Airborne Division and a division chief at U.S. SOCOM.

KELSEY SMITH, Lieutenant Colonel (LTC), has a bachelor's degree from Gonzaga University and master of military studies degree from the Marine Corps University. He has served in the U.S. Army for over 21 years as an Aviation Officer. He has deployed six times, serving in Afghanistan and Iraq in support of Operations ENDURING FREEDOM, IRAQI FREEDOM, and NEW DAWN. LTC Smith recently served as the Senior Aviation Trainer for the National Training Center at Fort Irwin, California.

U.S. ARMY WAR COLLEGE

Major General William E. Rapp
Commandant

*****

STRATEGIC STUDIES INSTITUTE
and
U.S. ARMY WAR COLLEGE PRESS

Director
Professor Douglas C. Lovelace, Jr.

Director of Research
Dr. Steven K. Metz

Principal Author and Project Director
Mr. Nathan P. Freier

Contributing Authors
Colonel (Ret.) Christopher M. Bado
Dr. Christopher J. Bolan
Colonel (Ret.) Robert S. Hume
Colonel J. Matthew Lissner

Contributing Researchers
Lieutenant Colonel Heather Bellusci
Lieutenant Colonel John R. Beurer
Colonel Ralph Borja
Mr. Steven Buelt
Mr. Michael Lechlitner
Lieutenant Colonel Robert D. Montz
Colonel Robert Phillips
Lieutenant Colonel Kelsey Smith

Editor for Production
Dr. James G. Pierce

Publications Assistant
Ms. Denise J. Kersting

*****

Composition
Mrs. Jennifer E. Nevil

Made in the USA
Monee, IL
11 August 2022